HANDBOOK
OF
ROCK GARDENING

Edited by
John Good Ph.D.

ALPINE GARDEN SOCIETY

First published 1963
Second edition 1988
ISBN 0 900048 46 8
© Alpine Garden Society
Lye End Link
St. John's
Woking
Surrey GU21 1SW

Photo Credits

AGS Library: 1, 2, 5, 6, 10, 18; Mike Ireland: 11; David Mowle: 12; Phil Phillips:
cover; Robert Rolfe: 3, 8; Barry Starling: 17; Stan Taylor: 13, 14, 15; Michael
Upward: 4, 7, 9, 16

Printed by L. Baker (Printers) Ltd.
71 Lombard St., Birmingham B12 0QU

Handbook of Rock Gardening

Contents

Introduction 7
The Joys of Alpines, by Joy Hulme 9
Starting with Alpines, by Joe Elliott 19
Soils and Composts, by Duncan Lowe 23
Propagation of Alpines, by John Good 29
Pest and Diseases, by Lionel Bacon 45
Rock Garden Construction, by W. K. Aslet 57
Alpines Without a Rock Garden, by David Mowle 63
Home-made Troughs, by Sid Lilley & John Good 72
Cushions, by Stan Taylor 78
Bulbs for the Bleak Days, by Jack Elliott 85
Sterling Silvers, by Chris Norton 89
Shrubs for All Seasons, by Barry Starling 94
Why Grow Dwarf Conifers? by A. R. Woodliffe 99
Plants for Shady Corners, by Richard Bird 102
Alpine Pilgrimages, by Michael Upward 112
Photographing Alpines, by Phil Phillips 123
Alpine Bookshelf, by Michael Upward 136
Index 141

Illustrations

opposite page

1. *Ranunculus glacialis*   16
2. *Primula bhutanica*   17
3. *Hepatica nobilis*   17
4. *Primula parryi*   32
5. *Ramonda myconi*   33
6. *Eritrichium nanum*   33
7. *Thlaspi rotundifolia*   48
8. *Gentiana brachyphylla*   48
9. *Cyclamen repandum*   49
10. *Galanthus ikariae*   64
11. *Erythronium* 'White Beauty'   64
12. *Narcissus* 'Jack Snipe'   65
13. Plunge frame in summer   80
14. Saxifrages in tufa   81
15. *Dionysia lamingtonii*   81
16. *Saxifrage oppositifolia*   96
17. *Kalmiopsis leachiana*   97
18. *Armeria caespitosa*   97

Introduction

The very fact that the first edition of this *Handbook* is now out of print after several impressions is testament enough to the continuing need for such a general guide to the fundamentals of rock gardening. This completely new edition retains only one chapter unaltered from the first, that about rock garden construction by the late master of the craft, Ken Aslett. Like its predecessor, it offers advice and guidance from some of the most experienced and successful alpine gardeners of our generation. They do not only tell how to grow this or that beauty of the mountains, however, important and helpful as that may be, but also convey the joy and pleasure in doing so. Throughout the book we are time and again taken to the mountain homes of the plants by those who have visited them, repeatedly, not just to track down this or that rarity amongst glorious scenery, although that can provide pleasure indeed, but also to study the plants in their habitats with an eye to determining their likes and dislikes and hence the most likely means of succeeding with them in cultivation.

Lest this suggests that alpine plants are, by nature, capricious aristocrats of the plant world demanding constant care and attention in the garden and thus not, perhaps, for you, it should be pointed out that the vast majority are easy going, hardy perennials which will grow and give satisfaction for many years if their few simple basic requirements are satisfied. These are spelled out simply but authoritatively in the pages which follow, which are chiefly devoted to these easy alpines. Because the chapters have been written independently by the different authors there is inevitably some repetition, but this serves only to highlight the more important points, such as the vital importance of good drainage.

There is nothing more annoying than to read glowing descriptions of plants that cannot be obtained for love or money. Nearly all of the plants mentioned here are widely available in the trade but some are not. All are in cultivation, however, and in my experience if you want them badly enough sooner or later you will acquire them! In doing so exchange will play an important part and the friendships built up in the process will, if you are like most gardeners, give as much pleasure as the plants themselves. There is also no better way of learning how to cultivate the more difficult alpines than by talking to successful growers. Often something quite simple, the moisture regime during the dormant season for example, spells the difference between success and failure.

The production of a book such as this depends on the willing co-operation of many people. The authors are to be thanked for making the book possible. In addition Sid Lilley kindly allowed me to alter and amend his excellent article on making troughs from the first edition. Duncan Lowe re-drew some of the line drawings from the first edition and kindly provided additional ones. Richard Bird, the Society's Joint Editor, read the whole of the draft and made helpful comments, especially on the layout. He also designed the cover. Mike Ireland, the Society's Colour Editor, helped in the selection of suitable transparencies for the colour plates and handled the colour printing.

John Good

The Joys of Alpines

by Joy Hulme

Alpines are joyous plants – a joy to grow and a joy to study. In their native mountains they have a brilliance and exuberance which stem from the necessity, imposed on them by the rigours of their environment, to spring into growth, flower and propagate themselves in the brief spell of summer. And as the grip of winter is loosened in successively higher regions, so the plants burst from their snow-covered dormancy, push their leaves and buds up through soil sodden from the melting snow and rich with the detritus of rock and animal and vegetable matter, to clothe the mountainsides with a gay kaleidoscope of colour which is unique in its beauty. For all of them, the season is short. Those that grow in the lush lower meadows are scythed down by early June and dried for winter fodder; those in the middle ranges, the alps proper, provide summer grazing pastures for sheep, cattle and goats, while the high alpines which grow in the uppermost screes and barren rocks are restricted to the short space of time between the melting of the last snow in late June and the first snowfall of winter which may sometimes be as early as August.

It is perhaps this urgent thrust to fulfilment, coupled with the pure, cool air of the mountains and the intensity of the ultra-violet rays at these altitudes, that give alpines their peculiarly attractive colours. Certainly it is the harshness of their environment which imposes on them their diminutive size and causes them to clothe themselves for protection in woolly or silky hairs, to huddle into cushion shapes to avoid the searing winds, to cling to crevices in rock outcrops or to anchor themselves with yard-long roots in screes. They will retain these properties in cultivation, given reasonably careful treatment, and show themselves thus to be among the most fascinating of all plants. Both as subjects for the garden and as the object of study in the mountains, they can be almost addictive, and the gardener who has once fallen under their spell rarely recovers from this obsession. For, unlike that heavenly choir of whom we sing that 'all their joys are one', the joys of alpines are legion.

Part of their charm lies, of course, in their smallness. Bigger is not inevitably better, and there is a delight to be found in tiny things that seldom fails to enthrall. The fabulous Easter eggs made by Carl Fabergé for the Russian Imperial family were renowned not solely for the jewelled workmanship of the casing, but because each contained a minute replica of a subject dear to the recipient's heart – a castle, a ship, a basket of flowers. Painting and sculpture in miniature have been an esteemed art form throughout the ages. The Japanese excel in the art of Bonsai and in the dwarfing of such plants as chrysanthemums. But alpines are as their conditions of life have made them, natural miniatures, with all the perfection of proportion that implies. Seldom more than 30cm high, often less than half that, they are mostly hardy, perennial and infinitely rewarding. They are, too, not merely natural miniatures, but in the main natural plants, for the hand of the hybridist has not fallen heavily upon them. There are, of course, well-known exceptions – the florists' cyclamen, Show auriculas, the many garden varieties of saxifrage, but by far the greater number of the alpines we grow remain as nature made them.

Even nature herself indulges sometimes in hybridising. *Primula glutinosa*, for example, a tiny plant from the Eastern Alps, with deep blue-violet flowers on 5–7.5cm stems, crosses readily with *Primula minima*, which bears bright rose-pink, deeply-lobed petals above a flat rosette of shiny, wedge-shaped leaves. They produce swarms of very similar hybrids, which are often difficult to distinguish from the parents. It is fun to spend some hours sorting through the offspring, but they do not rival the true *P. glutinosa*, one of the loveliest of primulas. To a large extent, therefore, alpine gardeners are basically purists, preferring the wild species as they grow in the hills, and knowing that seed from their plants will normally breed true.

Seed sowing brings another source of deep enjoyment to the enthusiastic grower. There is a special relationship between a plant grown from seed and the person who has nurtured it from its first emerging seedleaf to the mature plant flowering in garden or pot. A dreary winter day can be transformed into an exciting excursion into the mountains as seed lists are perused, dreams of exotic successes indulged in, and a final choice made among the many delights on offer. The Society alone lists over 4,000 different species, and there are related societies in Scotland, many European countries, North America, Australia, New Zealand, South Africa and Japan.

Alpines are for everyone; gone are the days when they were thought to need miniature mountain ranges built at vast expense. Provided a few basic requirements are borne in mind, many of them are very easily grown. The remaining chapters of this book deal fully with most aspects of rock gardening, but it cannot be too strongly stressed that their fundamental requirements are perfect drainage, a good soil with some humus in it, plenty of water in the growing season, and an open site away from the shade and drip of trees. Such conditions satisfy a multitude of easy species which can provide year-long interest with a minimum of work, except for the normal chores of weeding and watering in dry spells. In my own garden, there is a border about a metre and a half wide and some 12 metres long, with a mere 15cm slope from back to front. Admittedly it has the advantage of a good sandy loam, but its only other drainage is provided by a narrow trench between it and the lawn, filled with broken pots and rubble, and covered with soil. In spring and summer it is a riot of colour and in autumn and winter it remains gay and interesting with the many dwarf hardy bulbs planted around and under the perennials. Aubrieta, rock phlox, alyssum, campanulas, thymes, pulsatillas, dianthus, the less invasive oxalis, dwarf iris, primulas, and many others thrive in these simple conditions and rival in beauty many an herbaceous border requiring ten times as much work. In autumn the show is carried on by autumn-flowering crocus – *CC. nudiflorus, kotschyanus, pulchellus, cancellatus*, – by colchicum species, by the charming *Leucojum autumnale* with delicate white bells on slender reddish stems. Through the winter various forms of hardy cyclamen – *CC. coum, hederifolium, cilicium*, take over, to be followed by a wide range of snowdrops, charming little *Muscari azureus*, which is perhaps inclined to spread, but must be forgiven for the sake of its delightful china-blue flowers, by *Crocus chrysanthus, C. corcyrensis, C. tommasinianus* and many others, and by the spring snowflake, *Leucojum vernum*. It is a part of the garden which gives pleasure throughout the year.

These plants, rewarding as they are, are merely an initiation, for dedicated growers will go on to accept the challenge of the higher alpine species, and to house their chosen plants, with or without rocks, in raised beds, dry walls, on rock gardens, peat beds, in troughs, pots, frames and greenhouses. Then indeed the interest becomes universal, for all the mountains of the world render up their special treasures, and the ability to grow a particularly difficult or outstandingly lovely plant is a source of unalloyed pleasure equalled by few other gardening triumphs. The European Alps have long been renowned for the richness and beauty of their alpine flora, the Middle East is noted for its many bulbous species and as the home of such comparative newcomers as the dionysias, the vast resources of Russia are slowly being tapped, the great wealth of Himalayan plants is being brought back into cultivation, and Japan is a source of many rare and lovely things. The New World offers equal attractions for, while the treasures of the United States and Canada are comparatively well documented, the unique flora to be found in the mountains of South America is only now beginning to be appreciated. The other continents of the Southern Hemisphere all have their share of mountain plants, and the increasing ease and speed of travel to these remoter parts have brought further unusual alpines within reach of today's gardeners.

What could give greater pleasure than to succeed with the cultivation of a scarlet gentian from the Andes, to produce a flower-studded cushion of a difficult dionysia from Iran, a clump of the exquisite ice-blue flowers of *Primula bhutanica* or a pan of azure *Gentiana verna*? Air travel has undoubtedly made the world a smaller place and these distant mountains more readily available to many people. Who would have thought in the days of the Jesuit fathers in China, or the great plant collectors who operated in the first half of the present century, that there would be regular parties of tourists trekking up into the Himalayas and searching for plants on the very flanks of Everest itself? Who could have guessed that the wastes of Alaska and the Arctic would be opened up for their natural resources, enabling botanists to study the plants that survive over the permafrost? But all this and more is happening, and new exciting plants are still being found in the far corners of the earth. Iran and Afghanistan have yielded several new species of *Dionysia* in the post-war years and, although more skilled growers are learning to cope with this difficult genus, they are by no means yet in general cultivation. The immense wealth of plants in the vast range of the Andes is largely known to us only by repute. Seed is occasionally brought back, but few growers can boast of their splendid cruickshanksias, win prizes with their richly coloured Andean gentians, or exhibit superb specimens of the rosulate violas endemic to these volcanic slopes, with violet flowers peeping out from congested rosettes of thick little leaves. As recently as 1970 a new plant was discovered in the Southern Alps of New Zealand. Identified temporarily as *Clematis marmoraria* it is a tiny sub-shrub, spreading by underground suckers rather than climbing; its dark compound leaves make a perfect foil to the short-stemmed flowers of white or cream. In the world of alpines at least, all is not known and stereotyped; there are still fresh discoveries to be made, new plants to be studied, new skills to be learned, and the thrill of new triumphs to be achieved.

To the enjoyment of these challenges must be added other felicities. Alpine plants are a race apart, a race clinging determinedly to the stubborn independence which enabled them to survive in the rigorous conditions of the high mountains. Not for them the easy regularity that gives rows of symmetrical dahlias or greenhouses full of oversize chrysanthemums. They are individuals, not to be coaxed or bludgeoned into conformity or into accepting what is contrary to their nature. Apart from their basic demands for a good but well-drained soil and an open site, there are really no 'rules' for them, and they need to be known and studied intimately and to have their own special needs catered for. Such a relationship between grower and grown brings an endless source of interest and intellectual curiosity. Nature is infinite in her variety, and, since alpines include all types of plants, no limiting factor narrows the sphere in which the alpine gardener works. There exist miniature forms of conifers, flowering and fruiting trees and shrubs, bulbs in the widest sense of the term and, of course, annual and perennial plants, so that a very diverse range can be encompassed in a single trough or window-box. This type of gardening calls for more varied skills than are required to grow a row of Marigolds, and the alpine gardener is able to exercise his talents to the full in the smaller gardens of today. The days of large estates employing dozens of workers are basically over and most houses have small plots of land tended by their owners. Alpines fit perfectly into such a regime, furnishing a garden or greenhouse with colour throughout the year. A raised bed, simply and cheaply built, can contain hundreds of attractive miniature plants, further hundreds will enliven an unheated greenhouse, and a small terrace can be transformed by the careful use of troughs, sinks and carpeting plants. All through the winter months gardening can continue uninterrupted with a greenhouse. In nature alpines are kept dry and insulated under a blanket of snow, and some can only with difficulty survive our winters of rain and fluctuating temperatures. A greenhouse provides them with the protection they need, and a series of rewarding plants can be grown to give pleasure throughout the inclement months. Cyclamen species flower from autumn until late spring, the delicate dwarf daffodils from north Africa and southern Spain, brilliant tulips, crocus and iris from Europe and the Middle East, and ranunculus species from Lebanon and California will brighten dull winter days. These are all forms of gardening which give the grower total control over soil conditions, siting and watering, and enable him to satisfy the needs of many of the rarer and more unusual mountain plants.

The world-wide distribution of alpines is not, however, the sole international factor to give pleasure to the gardener, for alpine enthusiasts form a closely knit and friendly body of people. Any form of peaceful cooperation between nations must be valued for bringing closer ties between them, and high on the list of shared priorities must be a widespread concern for the preservation of natural amenities. The Alpine Garden Society and other related bodies have members in many countries of the world. They exchange seed, plants, visits and information. International conferences are arranged, members act in concert to help protect endangered species, to discover new plants and how to grow them, and they thus transcend all the artificial barriers that man imposes on himself. This continuing contact between people of like mind and the many-sided friendships that ensue bring an added dimension of enjoyment and a greater understanding of, and sympathy for, people of other cultures. What could exemplify this better than an extract from a letter recently received from a friend behind the Iron Curtain – "I hope that as free plantsmen you will struggle better, having more time for intimate touches with our small green and silver friends. Yes, life is great pleasure when your heart is able to spread through hearts of another individuals".

But perhaps the greatest joy of all is to see these lovely plants growing in their high, remote natural habitats. Mountains are stupendous things; not for nothing has man throughout the ages called them the homes of the gods. They have a power, a majesty and a beauty which can reduce man to his appropriate puny place in the universe. Yet it is here, among the eternal snows, the moving screes, the stark cliffs and the warming summer sun that alpines have their home, and it is here that they achieve their full beauty. Their loveliness in pots or rock garden is as nothing compared with their startling beauty in the mountains. To walk across a high pasture studded with the pure and brilliant blue of countless gentians, to climb to a distant haze and find a huge expanse of the creeping azalea in full bloom, to stumble on a damp hollow white as snow with a drift of golden-centred mountain Buttercups, to see a bare cliff dotted with the flower-decked cushions of *Androsace helvetica*, are unforgettable experiences. There is a long hanging valley high in the French Alps which, in spring, is white with hundreds of thousands of *Narcissus poeticus*, and there are meadows in the Dolomites ablaze with a myriad upturned cups of orange *Lilium croceum*. I have been up at 3,250m on Piz Corvatz in Switzerland, with international ski-jumping competitions taking place in sub-zero temperatures, and over a small rock warmed by the mountain sun the dazzling white cups of *Ranunculus glacialis* lay open above a rosette of fleshy grey-green leaves, while rosy tuffets of *Primula hirsuta* decked the precipitous rocks below. To the alpine enthusiast, a day spent among these bright jewels is one of unparalleled joy. The going may be arduous, but the rewards are great. For those less able to take strenuous exercise, there are many roads driving high into the mountains, and the popularity of ski-ing brings a proliferation of chair lifts and teleferiques. A well-known tourist spot may have a car park full to overflowing and a throng of visitors at a viewpoint, but let the canny flower-seeker walk a mere couple of hundred metres, and he will be alone with the flowers, the birds and the animals. The Vial del Pan in the Dolomites, the high-level track facing the magnificent glacier of the Marmolada, can be as busy as a London street on a sunny day. Hordes of noisy tourists, clad in a regulation gear of red and white socks, lederhosen, Tyrolean hats and brand new boots, stagger a few yards along the track, have their photographs taken against the impressive background of the highest peak in the Dolomites, then clamber back into their coaches and drive away. A few more hardened walkers venture on as far as the old refuge. But you can diverge a mere fraction from the path and find peace and solitude on a large rock, where none but the connoiseur goes to study the azure-flowered silky-haired cushions of the King of the Alps, *Eritrichium nanum*. In the lonely places of the mountains the world is as it was when it was young and unspoiled, and man can be at one with nature. I remember scrambling up a steep slope where, as I cleared the ridge, I came face to face with a young marmot. We were both so surprised that we froze, remaining motionless for several moments, then he turned his back on me and ambled calmly off.

On another occasion, we sat with Golden Eagles soaring overhead and watched them feeding a chick as large as a Christmas turkey on a rock not far away. And again, coming down one evening from the summit of Piz Naïr, we missed the last train and walked down in the dusk, coming to the lower woods among a band of grazing deer who paid not the slightest attention to us – they had clearly learnt the timetable by heart and reckoned that all intrusive humans had departed by that hour and the mountains belonged again to them.

Wordsworth, writing of Lakeland daffodils, says that "they flash upon the inward eye that is the bliss of solitude". We have an advantage denied to the poet, for we can capture the beauty of the flowers and the scenery on film. During dull winter evenings, we relive our holidays in the mountains, see again the lovely flowers that grow there, and recall small adventures that befell us. One day we indulged in some light-hearted banter with a coach-trip operator as to the only possible way in which to see the mountains – for us, on foot; for him, by coach. Next morning, we set out to walk through the woods and over the higher slopes to the top of the pass. Little more than halfway up, the heavens opened, and by the time we reached our goal, we were soaked to the skin. We decided to descend by the road rather than the sodden path, but had barely set off when we were overtaken by our coach driver friend. Laughing triumphantly, he insisted on giving us a lift, and two muddy and bedraggled walkers were shepherded into the midst of a coachload of immaculate tourists. They accepted us willingly, however, and plied us with chocolates and hot coffee, fearing, no doubt, that we might expire before their very eyes.

These pleasures will be with us for ever, as will yet another sedentary happiness – that of reading about the plants and the places in which they live. The early plant hunters, and indeed some of the modern ones too, led lives that for sheer excitement beat many of the most romantic adventure stories hollow. They brought back a multitude of plants, some of which are only now being re-introduced to cultivation. Their accounts of flowers, of scenery, of people, provide rich entertainment. Reginald Farrer, who wrote what is perhaps the Bible of alpine gardening, excelled

1. *Ranunculus glacialis*

2. *Primula bhutanica*

3. *Hepatica nobilis*

in describing the plants and their needs, and, although his work abounds in purple passages, he brings his subject to life in a way that few writers have done. Here is his description of *Saxifraga florulenta*, a rare endemic from the Maritime Alps. "It is a tragic and splendid old species, lingering on alone in the gaunt cold precipices. There in the stark red-grey walls it hangs, making a broad rosette of almost uncanny splendour, with glassy-smooth leaves, quite narrow, and of perfect brilliant green without the least touch of beading or silver, stiff and hard and sharply ciliated at their edges, running out into a point so acute that a healthy tuft is as prickly and ticklish to handle as holly or a bough of gorse . . . It always remains incurved like an angry dark green sea anemone, and never begins to unfurl its foliage until the moment comes for it to flower and die". Who could resist looking for such a plant? We could not, and we have searched for and found it in several places. An unknown valley in Italy seemed likely to provide another possible location for this rare plant. We drove up a long rough track, parked near a small refuge, and spent a fruitless day searching for the Saxifrage, perpetually frustrated by deep snow from climbing to the rocks where we felt sure it would grow. Back at the car, we were intrigued by the sight of a large man of commanding presence haranguing a crowd of young people at the refuge. To our surprise, he came over to us, inviting us to come and sample the liqueurs he made from alpine herbs. After this wine tasting, he showed us round his 'garden', an ancient moraine where he cultivated numerous forms of *Artemisia*, and then announced that we must see his great treasure, the rarest plant in the mountains. I asked, "Would it by any chance be *Saxifraga florulenta*?" He stared unbelievingly for a moment, gave a great shout of delight, and clasped my hands ecstatically, saying that we were the only people who had ever known of its existence. And there, cemented into the grotto-like rockwork of a shrine to the Virgin, were dozens of the saxifrage we had failed to find.

My gardening interest began, as many do, with annuals, perennials and herbaceous borders. Then one day a French friend invited us to share a holiday in his cottage in the Pyrenees. I was lost from that moment, overwhelmed by the unknown and lovely plants I saw around me. For over twenty years I have been under their spell, and I see no likelihood of a cure. One sunny morning in the Dolomites, we took the earliest teleferique up to the crest of Catinaccio. The only other passenger was an Italian workman carrying up cement for some repair work. Learning that we were English, he mentioned a town near where we live in Surrey. "I was a prisoner of war there", he said, "and it was paradise". We looked at the colours of the alpine flowers in the rocks and turf beneath the cabin, and thought that this surely was more a paradise than a dormitory town in England. But perhaps after all we have the best of both worlds, seeing the mountains in their full beauty and then growing, for the whole year round, these plants which are a challenge certainly, but also "a joy for ever".

Starting with Alpines

by Joe Elliott

Probably many people who are now dedicated alpine plant enthusiasts got their first impulse to grow these marvellously varied plants after visiting one of the many shows which our Society stages in various parts of the country. It must be a revelation for a newcomer to gaze on those remarkable pots and pans of perfectly grown specimens, many so covered with flowers that the foliage is hardly visible. The sad thing is that few of these show plants would be the most suitable for a beginner to start with. On the whole most – not all, but most – of the show bench plants tend to be those which need special skills to bring them to the perfection in which they are shown to the public and judges.

One of the main attractions of the broad band of plants which shelter under the umbrella heading "Alpines" is their variety and the varied conditions they require for satisfactory growth. Many are perfectly easy, reliable garden plants, but at the other end of the scale there are those which require constant and dedicated attention in the most esoteric soils and growing conditions. Apart from their intrinsic beauty this is one of their main attractions and none of us who have been involved with them for some years would have it otherwise.

That being so, the most sensible way for someone newly infected with the alpine bug is not to yearn immediately for the glories of the show bench but to start off with some of the more reliable, but still immensely varied, plants; learn from them and work up gradually to the more difficult ones and the day when you are awarded your first Farrer Medal for the best plant in the show!

One of the most constantly heard moans from uninitiated people with "rockeries" (dreadful word, which I am sure no self-respecting AGS Member would ever use!) is that all the flowers come in the spring, leaving the area drab and colourless for the rest of the year. This is nonsense, for with a little planning you can have colour and interest in rock garden, raised bed, trough garden – grow them as you will – for most months of the year.

The plants mentioned here are a highly subjective choice and only touch the fringes of what is available. There are at least a thousand more which could equally well be recommended to someone starting a collection, but these should all be fairly easily available and should all grow without difficulty in any reasonable well drained soil in a sunny situation.

One of the first to bloom, in March and April, is *Arabis ferdinandi-coburgii* 'Variegata'. To be honest the flowers are not all that impressive – ten to a dozen small white blooms carried on 15cm stems – but they *are* early and plentiful and the rest of the plant is highly decorative throughout the year. It forms a slowly expanding carpet no more than 2.5cm high of narrow leaves gaily striped in green and white; an all the year round asset. At about the same time, or soon after, *Aethionema* 'Warley Rose' starts blooming, with blunt rounded heads of clear pink flowers like miniature Candytuft. This plant too has a lasting appeal for its habit is to form a woody 15cm sub-shrub, well clothed in small leaves of striking glaucous blue-grey. It loves sun and has a nice habit of producing odd flowers throughout the summer.

Not long after these two *Erinus alpinus* starts its performance. As a wildling the little 10cm spikes of flowers are generally mauve but much more colourful than the type plants are the two forms 'Dr. Hanaele' and 'Mrs. Boyle', great improvements in bright red and rose pink respectively. There is also a white form, 'Albus'. All have a long flowering period and will sow themselves about in a most generous way, generally coming true to colour if kept apart. However, a rainbow mixture is more than acceptable. Individual plants are not usually very long-lived – two or three years perhaps, depending on season and situation – but once you have this plant your garden is unlikely ever to be without it.

Next in succession during May and June come the creeping phloxes. Among the most commonly grown are forms and hybrids of *Phlox subulata* and *P. douglasii*. Though they vary in size and vigour, as a general rule the subulatas are the larger and stronger growers, ideal for cascading down a bank or over a rock and producing spectacular carpets in all shades of pink, white, scarlet, crimson and lavender blue. The douglasiis are rather smaller and more restrained, so are suitable where space is more limited, such as in a trough garden. The colour range here too is wide. With both kinds the best thing is to buy the named varieties in flower so that you make sure of getting the colours which most appeal to you. They are always pot grown and will not resent being planted whilst in bloom.

The saxifrages are another vast and immensely varied genus. The group which are commonly known as "Silvers" could be said to be the backbone of any rock garden, ideal for growing in narrow crevices between rocks to form a living mortar of brilliantly silver leaves which are evergreen to give round the year pleasure. Most have arching sprays of white or creamy-white blooms in May, which may be anything from 10 to 45cm long. Some of the best forms are *Saxifraga cochlearis* 'Major', *S.* x *burnatii*, *S.* 'Esther', *S.callosa*, *S. cotyledon*, but there are many others, all of them hardy and reliable.

In June the dianthus come into their own; another large genus containing many dwarf plants suitable for the rock garden. Two of my favourites are *D.* 'Pike's Pink', a most willing grower and free flowerer with small double blooms of soft pink on 10cm stems over a neat grey carpet of foliage, and *D. squarrosus* with sweetly scented creamy white flowers whose petals are deeply fringed at their edges.

A bit later in the month and carrying on into July and August the campanulas start their parade. For sheer vigour, longevity and length of flowering period none can excel *C. muralis*; but it does need room to spread itself so don't plant it too near less robust neighbours. The flowers are lavender blue and bell shaped. Slightly less of a ramper with a mass of star shaped blooms nearer to a true blue in colour is *C. garganica*. Then there are the more Harebell-like members of the family of which *C. cochlearifola* is one of the loveliest. There are many forms – 'Miranda', 'Miss Wilmott' and others – all running gently underground threading their way through other plants without doing any harm except to the most delicate treasures. The little bell shaped blooms in various shades of blue hang from stems no more than 5 to 10cm high. *Campanula* 'Hallii' is a pretty pure white form.

Mention the word Gentian to a certain type of uninitiated gardener and a look of terror comes into his or her eyes. This feeling is quite unjustified. Though there are some tricky and wayward gentians and a few which you can't grow if your soil is limey, there are many which are reliable, easy to grow plants and none more so than *Gentiana septemfida* which with no trouble at all will give you a wonderful splash of true blue in July and August. It may take two or three years to attain its full impact, producing more flowers each year before retiring to a neat crown of ground-level buds for the winter. It will do this in any sunny soil which is not pure clay or desert sand.

For colour in September and October few plants give better value than *Sedum cauticola*. It spends the spring and summer producing 15cm arching sprays of rounded dove grey fleshy leaves which are most decorative; then in about mid-September has 7cm wide flat heads of vivid red flowers. Even later in autumn comes *Polygonum vaccinifolium* making a forest of little pink candle-like spikes composed of tiny pink flowers tightly clustered around the top 7cm of the 15cm stems. At the first sharp frost these turn a glowing russett colour, remaining decorative for many weeks. It is a creeping shrub, never happier than when tumbling over a rock or draping itself down a wall. Another spectacular late autumn flower is *Zauschneria californica*, a rabid sun lover which has a long succession of 2.5cm vivid orange-scarlet tubular flowers.

In the limited space available it has been possible to mention only a tiny fraction of the many thousands of alpines which will give you year round colour and interest. I hope that it has shown you that they are not all spring flowers and that colour and interest are possible at least from March to October. If you have already been infected by the alpine bug don't try to resist it: no branch of gardening is more wide ranging, rewarding and totally absorbing.

Soils and Composts

by Duncan Lowe

The mountains provide a variety of homes for the plants that live among them. There are crags, screes, ridges, meadows and marshes, all of which are inhabited by some of the species we call alpines. It follows that there can be no such thing as a "typical mountain soil", in fact, *soil* becomes more and more scarce with increase in altitude until, on the heights, there is none to be found, yet certain flowers bloom there and nowhere else.

It is only a relatively short time that we have been cultivating alpines, compared with trees, shrubs, herbs etc., but quite early it became clear that attempting to imitate the earth in which the plants were growing in their natural homes was not necessarily the best basis for cultivation. The climatic conditions of the garden are so different from those of the mountain ranges that the plants may modify rooting and feeding behaviour to cope with the changed environment; for instance, a crevice in an alpine cliff may be metres deep and constantly moistened by seepage, whereas one contrived between two stones in the rock garden will be shallow and easily dried out. Lodged in its artificial cleft the cultivated plant must send its roots downwards instead of inwards to find reliable water supplies and it will usually encounter far richer food supplies than in its native fractured rock.

Over the years (influenced by observations in the wild) we have experimented with composts, and, from trial, error and the occasional happy accident, a few dependable mixtures have emerged to become accepted for general use. They embody the important characteristics of the natural materials. They are open in structure to allow the rapid draining away of excess water, but contain sufficient fibrous substances to remain adequately moist. They are not rich in plant food (particularly nitrogen), but provide a sufficient and balanced amount *and*, in practical terms, they are made up from materials that are realistically obtainable.

There are really only two ways of housing alpines; they are either planted out in specially prepared garden beds or grown in containers (pots, troughs etc.), and the manner in which the planting mixture is prepared depends on whether it is for the bed or the pot. Whilst a carefully proportioned and refined compost can be made up to fill a few pots or seed pans, it would be impractical to produce a ton or so for the rock garden, which is why the soils and composts now to be discussed are in two categories, those for the garden and those for potting.

Garden mixtures

A great deal depends upon the nature of the ground that the garden occupies; if the native soil is reasonably fertile and well drained, but not quickly dried out, then a good number of alpines will flourish in it without further assistance. Few of us are blessed with such earth however and must modify, even discard, whatever the plot offers. Clays are wet and cold whereas sands are warm and dry; neither is suited to many alpine species. They both require labour and materials to improve their characters.

There is a hard way and an easy way to treat heavy soils, including clays, and of the two the easy way can be more effective in terms of suiting the truly alpine species.

The hard way is to break up the dense, sticky composition by mixing in anything that will open up the structure, letting the water out and the air in. Grit, gravel, peat, hop manure, and even the filling from old "flock" mattresses will help, but great quantities are required and the labour of digging and mixing them thoroughly with the earth is arduous. The volume of lightening material must be at least equal to that of the earth to be treated if the soil is really heavy. Even then it could fail if the plot is level, because water will then lie on the untouched sub-soil unless channelled and piped to a reliable drain.

The easy way requires only a light forking of the ground surface, after which it is covered with a layer of coarse gravel or small chippings to a depth of approximately 15cm (6″). There is a technique for planting in such shingles, and it requires the root ball of the plant to be worked loose until the roots can be widely spread. A hole is then scraped out to take the roots after which the gravel is gently pushed back to cover them. A watchful eye on the weather and generous response with the watering can for the first few weeks after planting is necessary until the plant recovers, but it will soon find and use, to whatever extent it wants, the solid earth below.

The light soils that lie over sands and chalks are usually superbly drained but lack the fibrous and jelly-like substances (humus) that both store moisture and provide plant nutrients. As a result they dry out rapidly and hold little nourishment. For high alpines (scree and crevice dwellers) the meagre food supply is less of a problem than the parching of their roots in dry periods, but the hungrier meadow plants will suffer equally from both of these shortcomings. To rectify the dryness much organic material must be added, peat or composted bark being the ideal materials, but, as for heavy soils, the amount of corrective material required is often underestimated. For each barrow load of soil up to half a barrow of organic material can be needed to produce worthwhile, lasting results. Even so it will be absorbed and broken down more quickly in light soils and needs to be topped up every three or four years. Sustenance for the plants has to be introduced, and preferably in a long lasting form. Bone meal, hoof and horn meal and thoroughly rotted compost or manure, sparingly added to the mix, are preferable to liquid feeds and other quick-acting fertilizers.

Raised beds are built principally to achieve the all-important drainage and they can be filled with a variety of mixtures to suit their occupants. If high alpines, then a 2 to 1 or 3 to 1 mixture of chippings or gravel to good soil, leafmould or a blend of either or both with peat will produce equally good results. Meadow plants and those from the grassy slopes will benefit from a rather richer diet, a typical mixture being half and half.

The peat bed, as it has come to be called, is constructed to suit a range of plants that have in common a need to root in spongy earth containing a high level of decomposing vegetation. By its nature this material is highly retentive of moisture yet free draining and open, due to its fibrous composition, consequently it satisfies not just peat-dwelling plants but a host of ericaceous species, woodlanders and moist ground plants.

For such plantings leafmould (barring that from chalky soils) is almost sufficient in itself, needing only about 20% of coarse sand mixed into it to ensure that drainage is excellent. Good leafmould, in quantities sufficient for garden bed construction, can be hard or even impossible to obtain and alternatives must be devised. Peat, composted bark and bracken litter all have adequate structure and mechanical properties but contain little nutrient. This can be rectified by adding plant foods in the form of chemical fertilizers, as is done to produce the now widely used peat-based composts, but this food is quickly exhausted and for long term plantings more substantial preparations are needed. Good light, lime-free soil mixed with an equal quantity of peat or bark is quite successful, as is the more rustic blend of 4 parts of peat to 1 part of dried and crumbled cow pats.

Potting mixtures

In the relatively small batches prepared for potting, seed sowing, trough filling etc., mixtures can be precisely made up and, unfortunately, this had led to the build-up of a mystique involving "essential ingredients", secret additives and mathematical proportioning. A visit to the mountains soon dispels such hocus pocus, for there it will be seen that the plants do not demand exactness in the constituents of the stuff that they root in.

There are no ideal mixtures – a compost perfected in the south-east of England might well prove to be too moisture retentive in the wetter north-west regions. Similarly, a mixture proved successful where porous, quick-drying clay pots are used can be over-wet in plastic pots. Trial and error are the only means of achieving reliable judgment in producing successful mixtures but there are basic recipes that will give encouraging results in a variety of containers and climates. These "old reliables" are frequently used by experienced growers as a first try when handling newly-introduced species; they are simple and there are only three that are widely used.

The lean mixture. Devised to suit high altitude species and others that are found in stone piles, gravels, silts and rock crevices, it consists of 1 part of leafmould passed through a 6mm sieve and 3 parts 3mm gravel or chippings (parts measured by volume *not* weight). The result, as described by one grower using it for the first time is, "a heap of dirty gravel" – but it does produce results. Being very free draining this mixture requires watering more often than more "normal" composts. Similarly, more frequent potting on is necessary – at least once a year.

Aretian androsaces, the more difficult campanulas and dionysias are typical of the plants that have been successfully cultivated in this unlikely looking concoction.

The general mixture. It is likely that at least 75% of mountain plants will be content with this simple preparation. Equal quantities (by volume) of John Innes potting compost No. 1 and 3mm gravel or chippings, thoroughly mixed – that is all. Peat-based potting compost as an alternative to the J.I. No. 1 is inferior.

Kabschia saxifrages, gentians, European primulas, many bulbous plants, pulsatillas, dianthus, sempervivums, violas and drabas are just a sample of the numerous and various plants that will grow just as well in this mixture as in others specially contrived or scientifically blended. The only caution required, and it is a big "only", is in the choosing of John Innes compost: today's market proffers good, bad and indifferent mixtures, the main variable being the quality of the soil used. To comply with the John Innes formula the soil should in fact be loam (rotted turves) from good meadow land and with a pH of 6.5 to 7, but it very rarely is. The best that can be done to check the quality is to look at and *feel* the stuff. Dense compost of a uniform, fine consistency which remains in a tight clod when squeezed in the hand and then released should be rejected.

The humus mixture. This heading is a clumsy attempt to identify a compost that will satisfy: Asiatic primulas, rhododendrons, cassiopes and others of that ilk with comparable needs. The recommended mixtures are virtually the same as those used in the peat garden, but refined somewhat by sieving out the coarser materials.

The difficulties in sustaining long term growth in peat-based mixtures without recourse to liquid feeds or other fertilizer additions pose even more of a nuisance in pots than in garden beds. It is, therefore, well worth while going to the trouble of making or obtaining good quality leafmould, which is possible given the much smaller amounts required for potting purposes.

Special mixtures. No attempt has been made in this chapter to discuss or evaluate the numerous other mixtures in use. Much has been claimed and argued regarding their merits. A quite false and unnecessary complexity, which is probably largely unintentional, exists. For example, a grower may find the gravel bag empty when starting some urgent potting. A hurried search for an alternative produces an old crumbling brick, hand-made a century ago, that crushes easily to a useful looking grit. In it goes and the potted plants thrive and flower well a few weeks later, perhaps in time for one of them to win a "Farrer" at a Show. Another myth is born. The unusually good spring weather favouring that particular plant in that particular year is not taken into account and all the credit goes to the crushed, hand-made brick – an "essential ingredient" from then on.

Tufa is neither a compost nor a soil and so, strictly speaking, should not be included in this article. But it is a remarkable substance and is the one "special ingredient" that can satisfy certain difficult species when more conventional mixtures fail. Broken down into a rubble of dust-to-pea-sized lumps it may be used just as it is for potting, or a little leafmould can be added. *Campanula zoysii* and *Jankaea heldreichii* are typical of the plants that respond. Surprisingly, tufa dries out far less quickly than would be expected from its appearance, yet the drainage is perfect, which is likely to be one of the main reasons for its effectiveness.

It is hoped this chapter has held to simple advice and reasonable methods. The materials and techniques described will not suit all the plants cultivated in the alpine garden, frame and glasshouse, but many of them. It is left to the grower to adapt and modify them, where necessary, to best suit his particular conditions and methods.

Propagation of Alpines

by John Good

Any conversation between experienced alpine gardeners will inevitably, and usually sooner rather than later, turn to propagation. In no other branch of horticulture does the raising of plants, as distinct from the growing of them, take such an important place.

The reasons for this interest in, or near obsession with propagation, vary with the individual. For some, particularly those new to alpine gardening and with space to fill, economic necessity may dictate that the garden be furnished in this way. The individual rock plant bought at the nursery is, inevitably and rightly, much more expensive than the individual bedding plant or bulb, but may well cover less ground. Propagation from initial bought in plants, or from the kind offerings of friends, is the obvious answer.

For others, routine replacement of old, tender or, let's be frank, dead plants, is the chief stimulus to propagate, while for yet another group propagation is the only means of obtaining those choice plants they seek, many of which rarely if ever grace the pages of nurserymen's catalogues. A few seeds offered on a garden visit or a snippet or two begged at the end of a Show may represent a once in a lifetime chance to acquire some beauty which has, seemingly for ever, remained on your "wants" list.

The basic principles of propagation, whether from seed or by vegetative means, are relatively straightforward and easy to learn, and a high degree of success will be achieved if they are adhered to. Nevertheless, experimentation is half the fun in gardening and much remains to be learnt, particularly regarding the raising of the rarer or more difficult species, and it is undeniably true that the curious gardener makes the best propagator. The willingness to try some untried, even unlikely procedure may well lead to success with an "impossible" species. And here I would make a plea that all the results of such experiments be brought to the attention of others through the columns of the Bulletin. Get into the habit of keeping records of all that you do or, if time does not allow that, at least of what you do that is different from 'normal' practice, whether your own or that described in the literature.

Since alpine plants are still (thank goodness!) mainly wild species, and thus can be raised from seed with a high chance of resembling their seed parents, seed raising is the most important branch of alpine plant propagation.

Alpines from seed

Successfully raising alpines from seeds depends, for the most part, upon the observance of a few simple 'rules':

1.   Sow seed fresh wherever possible. It is natural for seed to lie in the soil awaiting the right conditions for germination, unnatural for it to lie in a packet in drawer or luncheon box. If it must be stored then keep it dry and cool. Inside a plastic box with a tightly fitting lid in a domestic refrigerator is good; on the mantleshelf or on the greenhouse bench is bad.

2.   Use a free-draining, sterilized compost. Loam-based composts are easier to manage than those based on peat and are definitely best for species which are slow to germinate (see my article in Bulletin vol. no. 181 for a list). This is because peat-based composts will run out of nutrients quickly, perhaps before germination, and the seedlings may well be starved before it is realised that they have germinated. In my experience good John Innes (J.I.) no. 1 compost mixed with equal volumes of sharp sand, gravel or 'Perlite' to improve the drainage, suits most species. There is a lot of bad J.I. about, mostly resulting from the use of poor quality loam and inadequate sterilization. The main reason for using sterilized compost is to avoid the problem of weeds, which can be a real nuisance in seed pans, but sterile compost is also free of the many soil pests and diseases which can so easily overcome tiny seedlings. Remember that bought-in J.I. contains lime and therefore should not be used for lime-hating plants. Fortunately most of the latter are quick to germinate so can be raised in a lime-free, peat-based compost.

3.   Firm the compost well before sowing the seeds to provide a good supportive rooting medium.

4.   Sow the seed thinly on the surface of the compost and cover, but only just, with compost or grit. Sowing too deeply is a common

mistake and is especially harmful for very small seeds which must then use up much of their stored food reserves in growing through to the surface before they can start to photosynthesize. Grit as a surface dressing reduces problems with algae and liverworts which can easily choke small seedlings; it also protects the seed from rain splash in storms if the pots are to be kept outside without cover.

5.   Thoroughly wet the compost either by standing the container in a bowl so that the water is drawn up by capillary action until the surface is uniformly moist or water through a can fitted with a *very fine* rose. In the latter case be particularly careful to ensure that the pots are standing absolutely level as otherwise seed will be washed to one side of the pot resulting in uneven germination and high mortality.

6.   If in doubt as to germination requirements of a particular species, expose the seed containers to cold – the seed of many alpines is adapted to the cycles of warmth and cold associated with the montane environment and will not germinate until stimulated to do so by warmth following a cold period. Seed sown before the end of February in Britain and stood outside without protection should receive adequate chilling in most years and will then mostly germinate when the temperature warms up in spring. Seed received too late for this can be artificially chilled by mixing it with *damp* sand, Vermiculite or Perlite and placing it in a small polybag or phial in the cold (*not* freezing) compartment of a domestic refrigerator for about 6 weeks. The ideal temperature is somewhere between +2 and +5 degrees centigrade. The seed should be inspected regularly while in the refrigerator as some or all may germinate and it is essential that any seeds starting to show signs be immediately removed and sown in the usual way.

7.   Keep seed containers for at least three years as some species may take this long before any seed germinates while others will come up a few at a time over several seasons. When throwing out the compost from pots which have shown no germination, if possible put it on a bed where it can remain undisturbed for a season. Odd seedlings of rarities which had been given up as non-germinators have fallen to my trowel in this way.

8.   When the seedlings appear, thin those which are crowded with a pair of forceps and then water with a dilute fungicide solution. Overcrowding aids the spread of disease in seedlings as in people.

9.   Bait regularly for slugs and snails – every hardened gardener

has harrowing tales to tell of healthy potfuls of irreplaceable rarities lost to these persistent marauders.

10. Prick out when the seedlings are of a reasonable size to handle but before the roots have become inextricably intertwined. It is best to allow the seed compost to dry out for a few days before pricking out as it is much easier to separate the seedlings from semi-dry than from wet soil. Also, seedlings with very wet roots are difficult to prick out as they stick to the sides of the dibber hole rather than dropping nicely into it. A similar loam-based compost to that used for seed sowing but with J.I. no. 2 replacing the J.I. no. 1 is my standard mixture for pricking out. For woodlanders extra peat or sterilized leafmould is added to increase the sponginess and water-holding capacity while for high alpines the gravel is increased to 75% by volume of the mix to improve the drainage. Water the pricked-out seedlings carefully and keep them shaded from hot sun for about two weeks, gradually increasing the light and ventilation as they begin to grow. The stage immediately after pricking out is that when most seedlings are lost: particularly in the case of difficult species.

These 'rules' apply to the vast majority of alpines but there are some exceptions. Bulbs are generally best left in their seed pans for at least two seasons as many have relatively few roots which are brittle and easily damaged when pricking out. Regular feeding with a general purpose liquid fertilizer is recommended by many of the best growers who claim that the time taken to reach flowering size can be halved by this means. If the bulbs are not too crowded in the pot by this time it is probably better to plant out the contents of the pot or pan intact rather than separating them.

Large seeds, such as those of species peonies and daphnes, are generally best sown singly in small pots so that they do not have to be pricked out but can simply be potted on until ready to be planted out. While on the subject of peonies it is worth mentioning that they exhibit what is known as epicotyl dormancy. This means in practice that it is at least two years before the seedlings appear. In the first year a cold period followed by a warm period results in the growth of the seedling root only, production of the seedling shoot (epicotyl) being delayed until a further cold and warm period have passed. The seed can be persuaded to shorten this cycle by exposing it in a moistened condition to alternating cold and warm temperatures for periods of 12 weeks: a year is saved.

4. *Primula parryi*

5. *Ramonda myconi*

6. *Eritrichium nanum*

Very fine seed, such as that produced by many campanulas and their allies, may not manage to emerge through even a thin dressing of compost or chippings on germination. It can either be sown on the surface of the compost or, and this is better in my experience, on the surface of chippings overlying the compost. When watered the seed is drawn or washed down into the interstices between the gravel where it finds the ideal conditions for germination.

In addition to these very fine seeds which resent covering there are a good many species whose seeds require exposure to light after imbibition in order to germinate. Where it is known, this requirement is detailed in the list in my earlier Bulletin article referred to above. Such seeds need not be sown actually on the surface of the compost, although this is sensible if they are very small, but should be only very lightly covered.

One general point worth stressing is the need for cleanliness when raising plants from seed. Seed containers should be thoroughly cleaned before use and they should be stood on good clean gravel or similar to await germination. Watering should be with clean water and not with the contents of a water butt containing every sort of pest and disease. This may sound over fussy but much research has shown that seed and newly-germinated seedlings are particularly prone to attack. This is mainly because they have so little tissue and food reserves that infections or assaults by pests which would be withstood by larger plants are fatal to them.

Vegetative propagation of alpines

While seed is undoubtedly the most important starting point in building up an interesting and varied collection of alpines, giving the additional advantage of healthy, usually disease-free plants, there are good reasons for wishing to propagate many plants vegetatively. Some plants are so easy to propagate by simple division or from cuttings that it would be foolish to raise them from seed. Others while easily raised from seed are very slow to reach a reasonable size and may be much more quickly increased by vegetative means. Then of course there are the many named cultivars of wild species and also hybrids which can be raised true to name only by vegetative means. The practice of raising such plants from seed and distributing the seedlings under the seed parents' name, as if they were the real thing, is much to be deplored. At best the seedlings will closely resemble the parent; at worst they will be nothing like it. In either case the practice will, sooner or later, lead to the loss of the original variety from cultivation unless some determined nurseryman or hobbyist keeps the authentic plant and propagates it vegetatively.

The most widely used methods for vegetative propagation of alpine plants are division and the taking of stem cuttings. Leaf cuttings are used in a few cases as are root cuttings, layering and grafting so these techniques will also be briefly discussed.

Propagation by division. This is by far the simplest method of propagation as the divisions start with the tremendous advantage of having roots. Many plants can be propagated in this way, those producing wide mats of stems which root as they go being the easiest. Most campanulas, gentians, primulas, to name but three of the most important genera of plants for the alpine garden, can be increased in this way. Many of the more vigorous species and varieties may be simply dug up, divided and immediately replanted, requiring only careful attention to watering until they are re-established. Other more finicky types will need to be given protection in a frame or under a cloche until the shock of division with its partial root loss is overcome. In such cases partly severing the divisions some time before the final act will often greatly reduce the re-establishment period. The actual process of dividing a plant is best done with the bare hands. Having dug up a clump and shaken off most of the soil, which in itself will often result in the detachment of a few rooted pieces, pull the plant carefully but firmly apart. Do not be afraid to break major connecting shoots or roots but take care to ensure that all the divisions have a good amount of vigorous roots. If the divisions are known to be difficult to re-establish, line them out quickly in good well-drained soil in a frame, or put them in a pot or other suitable container and shade them from direct sun. Water thoroughly at first but do not over-water subsequently.

As to timing, division of easy subjects can be done at any time of year other than in the middle of a drought or when the ground is frozen. Having said that, spring and autumn are best, the latter season to be preferred if, like me, you are less assiduous than you should be with the watering can in cold, windy late spring weather. For more difficult subjects, spring is the better choice as the divisions then have a long period in which to re-grow before the next winter.

Propagation by stem cuttings. The basic problem in raising any plant from a cutting is that of maintaining its water and nutrient content while roots are formed. It stands to reason, therefore, that the more quickly the cutting can be rooted the better; also that the cutting must never be allowed to wilt and that it should be encouraged to make food by photosynthesis during the rooting period. In practice these requirements are met by choosing vigorous vegetative material for the cuttings which is in a physiological condition favourable to root formation and keeping it in a humid atmosphere but with adequate light for food production.

The greatest skill comes in selecting the material for propagation and in this case there is no real substitute for experience. As a general guide, however, cuttings are best taken from new but partially matured shoots in late spring or early summer. Such shoots are usually formed during or immediately after flower production and it is important that the new vegetative material and not the exhausted flowering shoots are chosen. In the case of woody species, cuttings are generally taken when semi-ripe, i.e. when the wood has begun to harden but before the shoot has lost its suppleness. In the case of late flowering species, non-flowering shoots are best but if, as is often the case, every shoot on the plant bears flower initials, remove these when making the cutting. In all cases great care should be taken to keep the cutting material turgid between collection and insertion in the frame, mist propagation bench, or other rooting accommodation. Old wives' tales about improved rooting resulting from leaving cuttings to partially dry out on the greenhouse bench are just that, old wives' tales.

The main points of controversy regarding preparation of the cutting relate to its size and whether it should consist solely of material of the current year's growth or should have a small proportion of older material at the base. The evidence on both points is far from adequate and there is room for further research. My own preference in general is for large cuttings because I like to get a large plant and I have obtained no evidence from my own work that such cuttings root less readily or produce less vigorous plants. As to the question of age of the cutting material, I prefer new material, and have never found that the possession of a 'heel' of older material helps rooting in any way.

One point which is well established is that cuttings of many plants tend to form roots more readily at a node (the point where a leaf or leaves join the stem) than at an internode. Thus in prepar-

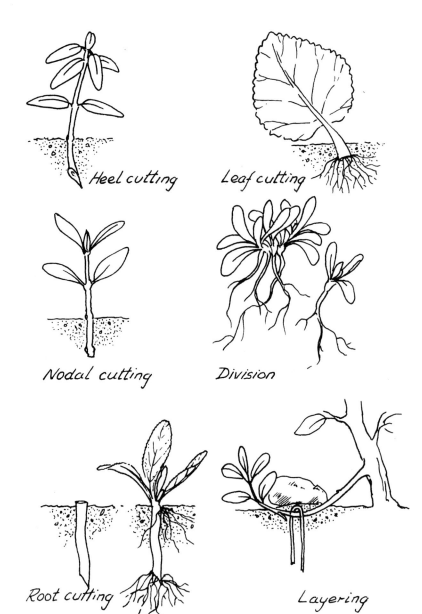

Heel cutting

Leaf cutting

Nodal cutting

Division

Root cutting

Layering

ing the cutting it is best to make the final cut just below the node. Leaves above the cut which would be buried in the cutting medium are best removed, but sufficient leaves should be left to provide the nutrients, hormones etc, needed for rooting.

Having mentioned hormones we might as well tackle the question of hormone rooting compounds. These artificial auxin hormones are the manufactured counterpart of natural hormones produced in the plant and involved in root initiation. They can be purchased in the form of either powders, in which case they are mixed with talc and usually contain a fungicide, or as liquids. In either case the active ingredients will be either naphthalene-acetic-acid (NAA) or indole-butyric-acid (IBA) or a mixture of both. The powders may be available in a variety of strengths, usually intended for softwood, semi-hardwood and hardwood cuttings respectively. The weakest is the one to use for alpines. In the case of liquids, different dilutions are usually recommended in the instructions, and again that recommended for softwood cuttings should normally be used. Whether it is necessary or advantageous to use such hormones at all is a moot point. My feeling is that if only a few cuttings are required and the subject is not expected to be difficult to root then there is little point in using them. If, on the other hand, a high rooting percentage is necessary or the subject is known to be difficult to root, it is probably worth resorting to hormones. My impression has been that in some cases the fungicide in rooting powder has had a more beneficial effect on rooting by preventing rot at the base of the cutting than has the hormone itself through root initiation.

Having prepared the cutting and either treated it or not with rooting hormone it is ready for insertion in the rooting medium. Again, various growers favour particular rooting media and what is best for you will probably largely depend on the moisture regime you adopt. If mist is used, and this is now well within the means of the amateur with the increasing availability of small-scale units specially developed for the home greenhouse, pure 2–5mm silica gravel is as good as anything. It is important that the gravel is well washed to remove fine material which would otherwise impede the essential free drainage. It is also important that it shall not be limey as many cuttings, not only of lime-hating plants, resent high pH in the rooting medium. Perlite or horticultural Vermiculite (expanded mica) can equally well be used but are more expensive, and Vermiculite is very messy to use, sticking to everything when wet and blowing everywhere when dry. Peat is not very suitable under mist as it rapidly becomes waterlogged and compacted and tends to keep the roots too wet. I only use it with mist for peat-loving plants, particularly dwarf ericaceae, and even then it is mixed 50:50 by volume with grit or Perlite.

If your moisture regime consists simply of limiting evaporation from the cuttings by any suitable means, from a special frame devoted to the purpose to a plastic covered seed tray or polythene bag supported over a pot by means of wire hoops, a more moisture retentive medium is advisable. A good general purpose mixture would be the half and half peat and gravel, mentioned above, with more peat for peat-loving plants and more gravel for those requir-ing sharp drainage. Demanding high alpines, such as cushion androsaces, dionysias, drabas, produce only very small cuttings which are best rooted in well-washed coarse silver sand. Some successful propagators of these and other difficult subjects fill the pot to three-quarters full with seed compost and top up with silver sand. The cuttings root in the sand and then the roots grow down into the compost so that the cuttings can be left until a well estab-lished young plant has been formed. Cuttings of these difficult species are likely to rot off very quickly if moisture remains on the leaves for any length of time so mist is inappropriate for them. They are usually put in either a closed propagator and given minimum watering to maintain turgidity or are left uncovered. In the latter case great care must be taken to ensure that the rooting medium is never allowed to dry out or to remain saturated and the cuttings must be adequately shaded.

On the question of shade, the best advice is to give the least shade necessary to prevent wilting and sunscorch. With mist very little if any shading is necessary as the wet leaf surface provides continual cooling by evaporation. In frames and propagators the amount of shade required can only be gained by experience and it is sensible to start with fairly heavy shading, reducing it experi-mentally until a minimum safe level is attained. Of course, cuttings rooted in the middle of summer will be much more likely to be scorched than those struck in spring or autumn and the season will also have an effect.

It is easy to forget the quality of the water used in retaining the moisture content of the cuttings. Very limey water inhibits the rooting of many genera and kills ericaceous cuttings, particularly under mist where the cuttings are continually exposed to a new dose of lime. If mist is used with such a high pH supply it may be necessary to install a water softener in the line. For smaller scale watering in limey areas, rainwater can be used, but check that it is not of high pH as many modern tiles as well as asbestos roofing materials contain cement, which is very rich in lime.

Having put your cuttings to root, leave well alone! It is very tempting to check them often for rooting by pulling them out of the medium, but this will at best lengthen the time taken to root and at worst prevent rooting altogether. Most cuttings will show clearly when they have rooted by producing new growth from the tips of the shoots. Similarly, most cuttings which are not going to root will quickly become unhealthy and may well fall prey to fungal attack. They should be removed to prevent the spread of disease to healthy neighbours. However, some cuttings, those of many hebes for example, can remain very green and healthy looking for months without producing either root or shoot, while other similar looking cuttings are well rooted and ready for potting.

Once the cuttings are well rooted pot them up into small pots using a similar mixture to that used when pricking out seedlings. Water them thoroughly and shade them for a few days to reduce the shock of transplanting before hardening them off for planting out or pot cultivation.

Leaf cuttings. There are very few alpines which are suitable subjects for leaf cuttings; sedums, ramondas and haberleas, Asiatic primulas, and lewisias being those most commonly attempted. In all except the sedums success usually depends upon there being a dormant bud attached to the very base of the leaf, which will produce a new plant. This bud may be so small when the leaf is detached as to be invisible to the naked eye but unless it is there failure is assured. For this reason the leaf should be detached as near as possible to the stem, either by slicing it off at the junction with a sharp blade or by pulling it sharply down and away from the stem so that it comes away cleanly with the bud intact. In the case of many sedums, roots can be formed anywhere on the leaf surface and most are very easy to increase in this way. The leaves are simply laid on the surface of normal cutting compost in a pot where they will often root in a few weeks. For more difficult subjects the leaves are shallowly inserted into the medium. Asiatic primulas, ramondas and haberleas take very well under mist but lewisias and most other possible subjects would be better kept in a closed case of some kind. Treatment of the plantlets once formed is the same as for seedlings, but do not be in too much of a hurry to separate the youngsters from their parent leaves until the latter are fully senescent and of no more use in providing food.

Root cuttings. It is certain that many more alpines could be propagated from root cuttings than are to-day. It is worth trying any plant which has proved difficult to propagate by more conventional means and which has the requisite fleshy roots. While fine fibrous roots may produce buds under some circumstances they are too fine to handle and plants bearing them are generally more easily propagated by other means. Many rosette plants, most of which have fleshy roots, are suitable for root cuttings. A good example is the little yellow flowered crucifer, *Morisia monanthos*, which behaves like a Dandelion, producing new shoots freely from severed roots. Another, much rarer example, is the beautiful white flowered *Weldenia candida* from extinct volcanoes in Mexico. This produces thick, very fleshy roots, which also very readily produce rosettes of leaves when damaged. If the plant is grown in a pot plunged in sand on the greenhouse staging the roots will, sooner or later, grow through the drainage hole into the sand. If the pot is then given a sharp twist before being lifted the roots will break off. Within a few weeks the root left in the sand will produce a new plant, or perhaps several, which can be teased out of the sand and potted up. This may sound a rather brutal method of propagation but, because the plant is in a pot and the rest of the root system is undisturbed, there is generally little or no setback to the parent.

For less easy subjects, which are of course the majority, the technique is to turn the plant out of its pot and remove one or two large healthy roots. This can most appropriately be done when the plant is due for potting on and so would be disturbed anyway. The severed roots should be clearly marked in some way to distinguish top from bottom as it is important that they are set in the rooting compost the right way up. The best way to do this is by making a slanting cut at one end and a straight one at the other. The roots should then be cut into sections about 2–4cm long, or if they are very thin, a little longer, again maintaining their correct orientation. They are then inserted in a pot which has been filled to within 5cm of the top with well firmed seed compost overlain with a thin layer (5mm) of sharp sand. Place them upright, quite closely together, with their bases in the thin layer of sand and fill the gaps between them with sand also so that the tops of the sections are about level with the surface. Water thoroughly with a fine rose and place the pot in a lightly shaded frame or below the staging in the alpine house. It should not be necessary to water again for some time, particularly if a plastic pot is used, and overwatering is certainly to be avoided. When the root cuttings have produced a good crop of healthy new leaves, gently knock the contents out of the pot to see how much new root development has taken place. If this seems adequate to support the new top growth, pot the new plants up individually, otherwise return the contents intact and leave for a further period.

Grafting. There are very few occasions when the alpine gardener need resort to grafting, but it is such a fascinating and rewarding propagation technique that some will occasionally have a go for fun as much as anything. Needless to say, it is used only for woody species, and then normally either for those which are very difficult to propagate by other means or of which very little propagation material is available. A particularly difficult to root but desirable dwarf *Rhododendron* or dwarf conifer, or a rare slow growing *Daphne,* for example.

There are three main things to consider when grafting: first, the stock (the part of the graft combination with roots, to which the desirable 'scion' is joined); second, the scion itself; third, the best time to do the job. The choice of stock may or may not be crucial; it is difficult or may even be impossible to know for some woody alpines which are only rarely grafted. The stock must, of course, be of the same genus as the scion, and preferably of as closely related a species as possible. In the case of genera containing both deciduous and evergreen species (e.g. *Daphne*) it is generally reckoned that like should be grafted with like but in practice I have found no difference in 'take' or subsequent vitality when evergreen or deciduous species have been used as stocks for grafting *Daphne petraea* 'Grandiflora'. The stocks should be young and vigorous and preferably specially grown for the purpose from seed. For ease of handling, particularly if very small plants are involved, it is best that the stock be pot grown. The scion material should also be vigorous, well ripened, and preferably of nearly the same stem diameter as that of the stock. This is so that as great

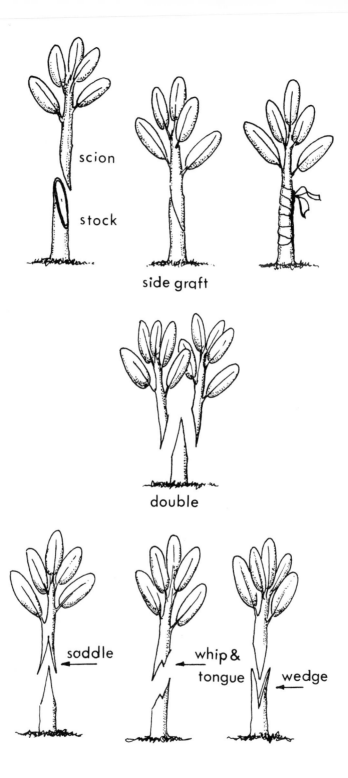

scion

stock

side graft

double

saddle

whip &
tongue

wedge

a part of the cambium (the tissue which unites scion to stock) of each component as possible is in contact. If the scion wood has to be kept for any length of time between collection and use it should be stored cool and damp, but not wet. It could be heeled in somewhere sheltered in the garden or put in canvas bags or similar in a domestic refrigerator where it will probably remain viable for several weeks. Which brings us to the question of timing. The best time for making most grafts is in early spring, just as the sap begins to rise but while the buds on the scions are still dormant. If the scion and stock are of different species and the scion comes into growth earlier than the stock it may help to bring the stock on a little by bringing it into gentle heat a few weeks before grafting takes place.

Various grafting techniques can be used (see opposite). In all cases it is best to make the graft as near as possible to the soil surface as this limits the amount of stock material from which undesirable shoots can arise. The simplest technique in most cases is the side graft in which matching slanting cuts are made on the top of the stock and the base of the scion, the two being held together with raffia, grafting tape or some suitable substitute. The chance of a successful take can be improved by making slanting cuts on either side of the severed top of the stock and binding on two scions. I have found the stretchy PTFE tape used by plumbers for sealing pipe unions to be a very good grafting tape. Whatever is used, the graft should be quite tightly bound to maintain close contact and prevent drying out. Grafting wax smeared over the raffia binding is the traditional way of assuring this but with PTFE tape it is unnecessary. The saddle graft (see opposite) is made in a similar way to the side graft except that, as the illustration shows, the scion sits like a saddle on the inverted 'V' cut formed at the tip of the stock. Clearly, this technique demands that the two be of closely similar diameters. I find it excellent for tiny grafts where the scion and stock are only as thick as matchsticks, since it is very difficult to get close contact with other types of graft. An equally good alternative to the inverted 'V' cut is a normal 'V' in which the scion sits in, rather than on the stock.

Having made the graft, place the pot in a shaded propagator or frame, preferably with a little heat if available, making sure that the compost in the pot never dries out nor becomes waterlogged, and that overheating is avoided. A sure sign that the graft is taking is the swelling of the union, especially if associated with vigorous new growth from the scion. Do not be anxious either to remove the binding material or to expose the plant too soon to extremes of temperature or humidity. Patience is especially virtuous where grafting is concerned! Remove shoots arising from the stock as they will tend to overpower the scion in the early stages if allowed to do so. Once the scion is growing vigorously it should suppress the buds on the stock, although occasionally the odd shoot may escape from domination and need to be removed.

Pest and Diseases

by Lionel Bacon

A garden is a highly complex living community – a vast range of plant life from the obvious weeds down to the invisible bacteria and viruses; and of animal life from mammals and birds through insects and worms to invisible protozoa. Most are harmless, some positively beneficial, and a few destructive to our plants. Most of them prey upon one another, so that there is an unstable, constantly changing, equilibrium. When we seek, for instance by the use of chemicals, to tilt this balance in favour of our plants, there is always a danger that the chain reaction may in the long run result in more harm than good.

Some creatures do both harm and good. Birds and butterflies are a delightful and welcome part of the garden scene: the former may tear spring flowers, but they also eat slugs, snails and insects. Cats may dig up the garden to make their deposits, and kill fledgling birds, but they also kill mice and voles. Wasps may attack fruit in the autumn, but they also eat insects. So weigh up the pros and cons, and give each creature the benefit of any doubt.

Most rock plants in the open garden have considerable reserves and powers of regeneration of roots and leaves, and so are relatively free from serious damage by pests and diseases; but tiny plants, such as seedlings, are at greater risk, and can be more readily protected in frames or plunge-beds. But bringing plants together in pots into an enclosed environment carries its own risks. Those in frames or alpine houses are more often found to be attacked by pests or diseases; and while this may in part be a false impression due to closer observation it is also true that some vermin, such for instance as aphids, flourish in enclosed conditions where they are protected from the elements and from natural predators, such as birds. Also, the bringing together of related plants in a 'collection' may facilitate the build-up of pests specific to these plants.

The best control lies in prevention. This means first good cultivation: healthy plants are more resistant to disease and better able to stand some loss of root or foliage. It means also good garden hygiene – the removal and destruction of dead, dying or diseased plants or foliage. It means continual watchfulness for the early signs of any sickness or infestation at a stage when it can be checked with minimal interference with the biological balance of the garden. Successful prevention depends also upon learning to know both one's plants and one's pests – to know which plants are most vulnerable to which pests, and when; and to learn the life-cycles and habits of the pests in one's own garden.

These preventative measures do not obviate the need to destroy pests, but they reduce this need, and enable it to be concentrated at the right time and place. 'Hit or miss' pest destruction is very much to be deprecated: it is expensive, it may be ineffective, or it may hit the wrong target and destroy not only the pests but also the natural predators – or even indeed damage the plants themselves. This is not to say that toxic chemicals have no place in the rock garden, and in the paragraphs that follow the use of chemicals in appropriate cases is recommended – but before destroying any creature, by chemical or any other means, please consider whether it is necessary to do so, or whether the 'cure' is worse than the disease; and, in resorting to chemicals, bring them to bear at the right place and the right time in the right dosage.

Animal Pests

Mammals. Fieldmice and voles are numerous in many gardens, and can be very damaging to small bulbs and tubers. They breed very rapidly, and it is important to be alert to signs of their presence – holes burrowed into the soil or between stones, shallow runs in the grass, bulbs thrown out, or crocus leaves lying where the corms have been devoured – and to trap immediately, before a population builds up. Cover the traps with sieves to keep out birds.

Moles do not feed on vegetation, but they throw plants out of the ground in the process of burrowing, and in dry weather this will quickly result in death. Their burrows among rock work can be very inaccessible, and provide homes for other small mammals. Try to trap them before they enter the rock garden, and be alert to the need to replant dislodged plants.

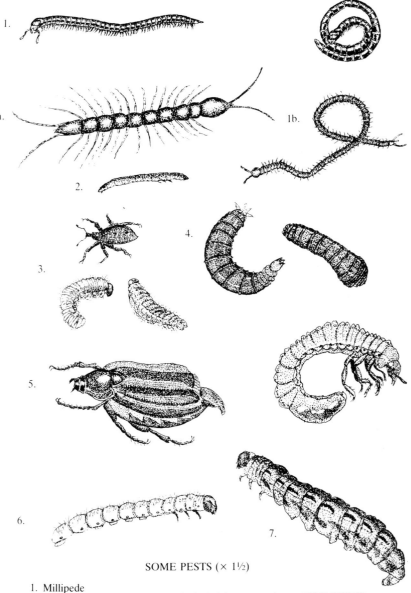

SOME PESTS (× 1½)

1. Millipede
1a, 1b. Two kinds of centipede, included for comparison – NOT PESTS)
2. Wireworm
3. Vine weevil and larvae
4. Leatherjackets
5. Cockchafer and larva
6. Swiftmoth
7. Cutworm

Mammals apart, it is convenient to divide animal pests into those which attack plants above ground and those which attack the roots, and as killers the latter are far more important.

Underground invertebrate pests. Some of these can be very serious, for they damage the plants at or below ground level, and if they emerge from the soil at all they are mainly nocturnal: the damage they cause can be fatal before it is detectable. The main offenders are cutworms, leather-jackets, wireworms, vine-weevils and ants.

Cutworms (illustrated p. 47) are the caterpillars of a group of related night-flying moths, of which the Yellow Underwing is the largest and probably the most widely distributed. They spend their day just below the surface of the soil, and at night emerge to feed, frequently eating right through young plant stems at the base.

Leather-jackets (illustrated p. 47) are the larvae of Crane-flies ('Daddy Longlegs') and they behave similarly to cutworms but in addition devour plants at the roots. They favour damp soil, and are common also in lawns.

Wireworms (illustrated p. 47), the larvae of Click beetles, are thin, tough-skinned orange (or whitish when smaller) creatures about 20mm long. They abound in some acid-soil areas, and can be found burrowing into the tubers of e.g. cyclamen in the rock garden, as well as into tuberous crops such as potatoes.

Vine-weevils (illustrated p.47) likewise seem to favour acid soils. The larva is a white grub up to 12mm long, soft-skinned, plump, tending to be curved into a comma shape and often lying head to tail when disturbed. It is very destructive to the roots of many plants, perhaps favouring most, members of the primula family, and can be devastating both in the garden and in pots. Whole beds of primulas can be lost in a very short time if the plants are not watched and action taken to destroy the pest as soon as signs of attack (wilting, poor growth, yellowing of the foliage) occur. The adults, like most other weevils, feed mainly at night, eating holes and notches out of leaves; but it is the underground damage of the larvae which is the more serious.

All these pests seem to have years of special abundance, depending no doubt on the fluctuating balance between them and their predators, which in turn are strongly influenced by climatic factors. A hard winter which results in the death of many insectivorous birds may, for example, result in a big build-up in numbers.

7. *Thlaspi rotundifolia*

8. *Gentiana brachyphylla*

9. *Cyclamen repandum*

There are other pests which, in most years, are less common, for instance the larvae of Cockchafers and the caterpillars of the Swift Moth – both underground root-feeders. With all of them, 'search and destroy': weeding and hand forking, and lifting and examining wilting or otherwise 'unhappy' plants, will help to keep down the population. But where infestation is heavy one may have to resort to chemical pesticides. There is a bewildering range of these, differing in their persistence (the length of time they remain active in the soil), in their effectiveness against the different kinds of vermin, and in their phytotoxicity, i.e. the poisoning effect that they may have on the plants themselves. HCH (=BHC, Lindane, Gammexane) is moderately persistent and effective and is not, I believe, injurious to most rockplants; but its use in areas to which birds have access should be limited and exceptional. When it is used, it should be in adequate dosage to avoid any risk of build-up of resistant populations of the pests.

Ants can be very destructive of plants, particularly on light (e.g. sandy or chalky) soils; and the structure of a rock garden favours colonization by the smaller species. Their activity, particularly above ground, waxes and wanes according to the season and weather, but below ground they are not completely inactive except perhaps in freezing weather. Often the first sign of an ants' nest is a dead plant. They seem to attack particularly the Caryophyllaceae (the Pink family), tunnelling through the soil between the roots. This probably promotes excessive drainage and hence a risk of dessication; but they appear to kill plants in a more positive way than this, perhaps by chewing through roots and underground stems in the process of burrowing, and perhaps also by exuding formic acid in the process. The reason for supposing this is the manner of death of the plants is that a branch or section dies and turns brown, the rest appearing at first healthy, but it is soon seen to lack vitality – cuttings from it do not root, and subsequently and inevitably it dies. Many methods of destroying ants' nests have been advocated; but by far the most effective in the writer's experience has been an Antkiller Dust (I.C.I.) containing Pirimiphos-methyl, dusted on and forked in as deeply as possible.

Earthworms in the garden should be treated as friends, aerating the soil and pulling down and digesting rotting foliage, but in pots they can be damaging. They feed on dead and decaying plant material, but no doubt in pots small roots are sucked in as well, and the soil of the pot becomes replaced by a clogged silt, which is the soil after it has passed through the worm's body. Perforated zinc over the drainage holes is of little use: small worms can penetrate it, and anyway worms can readily climb up the sides of pots and enter them from above. It is best to tip out the plants periodically and remove any worms, which is easier than it might seem as they are nearly always on the outside of the root ball, next to the pot. Likewise, great care should be taken to remove any worms from the root ball when potting on, and if unsterilized loam or leafmould is used in composts care should be taken to remove them from this also.

Above-ground invertebrate pests. Gastropods (slugs and snails) are of many kinds, varying in size, appearance, habits and habitats. Most species feed mainly on the green parts of plants (living, dying or dead), but some are carnivores and a few feed on other slugs. They feed mostly at night and are particularly active in humid weather in spring and autumn, although remaining very numerous and troublesome throughout wet summers. During the day they rest under the cover of foliage, stones or in the soil. Slugs are most damaging in frames or plunge-beds where there are small plants, and one individual can easily destroy many hundreds of seedlings in a short time if not detected and destroyed. In the rock garden a big build-up of gastropods can cause unsightly damage to many plants, but their feeding is selective so that the main problem is the destruction of a relatively few highly valued plants which are particularly attractive to them. Members of the daisy family, such as *Aster alpinus*, many of the smaller campanulas, *Omphalodes luciliae*, and alpine calceolarias are among those frequently attacked.

Slug pellets containing Metaldehyde, or the more persistent and rain-resistant Methiocarb, are effective, but Metaldehyde in particular is poisonous to birds, hedgehogs, frogs and toads, which may feed either on the bait itself or upon the poisoned slugs and snails. Cats and dogs, especially the former, may also be poisoned by eating the pellets. For these reasons heaps of pellets should not be placed where these animals can get access to them, but should be covered by pieces of glass or similar and should be removed along with the dead slugs and snails when their work is done. Less likely to be damaging to wild animals (including birds) and pets is the sprinkling of pellets at a low density in the parts of the garden where the need is established, with individual baiting only of those plants known to be particularly vulnerable to slug and snail damage. The writer has had no success with 'slug-pubs' – saucers or other containers filled with beer, but some gardeners swear by them. Go on killing gastropods wherever you find them, and the more you tend your garden – weeding, trimming, forking over, etc. – the more you will find and destroy. Watch out for the clusters of round, pearly, soft eggs. Remove decaying foliage; search under matted plants, e.g. aubrietas and arabis, where both slugs and snails tend to congregate. They are readily killed by dropping them into a jar of salt water – but change it often!

Aphids attack plants both above and below ground, but are predominantly pests of the green parts of plants. There are many different kinds, most of which can be lumped as greenflies, blackflies or root aphis. They are sucking insects, feeding upon the sap of plants. They breed at a phenomenal rate, and because of their vast numbers, can extract a very great deal of sap, causing distortion of the stems and leaves, and in the case of Root Aphis, wilting or death. Apart from this direct damage, disease viruses may be introduced through the punctures they make in the plants, and this can be more important than the sap loss. In the open garden, more so than in the alpine house, aphids are devoured by natural predators such as birds, ladybirds and Lacewing flies. However, some rock plants seem to be particularly prone to attack, and it is worthwhile getting to know which these are in one's own garden. Watch for leaf distortion, and in particular watch in the early spring for aphids which have over-wintered on plants in frames. Watch also for ants on plants: they are not attacking the aphids for you, but 'nursing' them and feeding on the sweet sticky 'honeydew' that they exude. Chemical treatment is the only really effective way of killing aphids but, as always, the problem is to kill the aphids but not their predators. There is a large range of chemicals, some acting by contact only, some systemically (i.e. by absorption into the plant so that the aphids are poisoned by the sap) and some combining the two methods of attack. The systemic chemicals are themselves poisonous to some plants and extra care should be taken when using them on a new subject for the first time. The less harmful but less effective (or at least less long-lasting) contact insecticides must of course contact all the aphids if they are to kill them and this is not easy to achieve; especially in the case of very dwarf or cushion plants. The writer uses I.C.I. Rapid Greenfly killer, which contains Pirimicarb and is claimed to be harmless to ladybirds and lacewings, on infested pot plants; and (rarely) in the garden upon individual heavily infested plants.

Many other kinds of creature feed on plant foliage, but rarely do much harm except to seedlings and other very small plants. Woodlice feed mainly on rotting vegetation at night, hiding by day in dark moist places, in crevices and under stones, so good rock garden construction and care will keep down the numbers: in frames they can be destroyed with HCH. Much the same applies to millipedes, though their numbers are usually much smaller; destroy when seen but do not confuse with the beneficial centipedes (illustrated p. 47). Leaf-eating caterpillars of a wide range of moths and butterflies can be found from time to time on rock plants, but usually only in small numbers. They can be left well alone or picked off by hand. In some years this or that species may suddenly become common and produce unsightly damage, necessitating a limited use of a Derris or Pyrethrum insecticide – but this is lethal also to bees. Similar considerations apply to other insects (some of them less lovable) including frog-hoppers and various kinds of beetle, chafer and weevil. Flea-beetles in their hundreds can cause unsightly blemishes, mainly on the leaves of crucifers, and may require the temporary and local use of an insecticide dust or spray.

Diseases

The term 'disease' is open to very wide interpretation, and could include all sorts of damage and injury, from the weather or otherwise. Here will be considered briefly the infections caused by the attacks of moulds and other fungi, bacteria and viruses; and diseases resulting from deficiency of certain minerals in the soil.

Infectious diseases. In the main, rock garden plants are not prone to infectious diseases: in alpine houses the risk is perhaps a little higher, though as with animal pests, this may be more apparent than real owing to the plants being under closer observation.

Moulds, other fungi and bacteria of a vast range of species abound in a garden, and are an essential part of its life: only very few are 'enemies'. Many kinds of fungi, whether those which can be seen by the naked eye or, as in many cases, microscopic, flourish on dead and dying plant tissues, so it should not be assumed that a dead plant with mould on it was killed by that mould. Nevertheless, some fungi do attack living plants, and the best preventive is good garden hygiene – removal of dead and dying plant tissues – so far as is practical. In general such material can safely be composted, but plants killed by any known specific disease are best burned. A list of the fungal and bacterial diseases of plants makes, at first sight, alarming reading – rusts and smuts, mildews and moulds, blisters and scabs, rots, spots and blights – a terrifying host. But when he turns to a list of the plants affected the rock gardener's peace of mind is restored. Furthermore, it is important to remember that plant diseases are much more widespread and difficult to control when many individuals of the host species are grown together, as in agriculture or commercial horticulture. The diversity of species which we cultivate in our gardens is very helpful in limiting disease problems. Nevertheless a few diseases, and particularly those which are not limited to one host species or a narrow range, may be troublesome, so we should be on guard.

Botrytis (Grey Mould) and other moulds are perhaps the most widespread and damaging diseases, often killing seedlings or unestablished cuttings, but also damaging, sometimes fatally, mature plants in frames or alpine houses. Over-watering, overcrowding and inadequate ventilation all increase the plants' vulnerability, but where humidity must be maintained (e.g. in cutting frames) fungicides are helpful. There are now many of these, several containing Benomyl as the active principle, but with many other active chemicals also available. Using them in rotation will help to prevent the build-up of strains of the fungi resistant to particular fungicides. As with insecticides, the use of these chemicals should be sparing and strictly according to the maker's instructions as to dosage.

Stored bulbs, corms and tubers are very vulnerable to attack by moulds, particularly if the bulbs are damaged at lifting or are stored in damp conditions. Additionally, some types are prone to specific diseases, such as Iris Ink Disease (in which the corms become blotched with the black spore bodies of the fungus) or Narcissus Basal Rot (in which the base of the bulb rots, preventing the growth of new roots). For infected bulbs growing in the garden there appears to be no effective treatment for these diseases other than clearing the area, burning infected bulbs, and not re-using the site for bulbs for at least three years. As a preventive measure, bulbs etc. lifted for storing, may be dipped in a fungicide solution such as Benomyl and then dried, or the treatment may be applied immediately before planting.

Viruses, the smallest of living creatures, if indeed they can be called such, are ubiquitous and are spread among plants in a variety of ways. The most common, already described when referring earlier to aphids, is by sucking insects, but they may be transmitted by nematodes (eelworms) in the soil and even by abrasive contact between one plant and another if the epidermal cells are damaged. Not surprisingly, it is very easy to transfer viruses from one plant to another during the normal processes of cultivation, particularly when propagating from diseased and healthy plants and using the same knife, razor-blade etc. Dipping the blade in alcohol and then passing it through a flame will sterilize it effectively and help to prevent cross infection. Despite a common misunderstanding to the contrary, some viruses can be transmitted through the seed, although this is the exception rather than the rule and most seedlings are free of viruses until infected from other plants.

Viruses produce many different symptoms, common among which are variegation in leaves and patches and streaks of abnormal colouring in flowers as well as assorted malformations, mottling and general debility. Much work is being done on the identification and characterisation of viruses in agriculture, commercial horticulture and forestry and in some cases (e.g. raspberries, strawberries) virus-free stock is produced routinely for purchase by growers and the amateur. Unfortunately, however, alpines being plants of little or no commercial interest, there is no chance of the extension of the appropriate propagation techniques to them. Furthermore, there is no effective means of destroying viruses in growing plants so that we must fall back on the destruction by burning of diseased plants, general cleanliness in the rock garden, and the control of aphids and other sucking insects, which, as we have repeatedly stressed, are necessary in any case to limit the build-up of the more tractable fungal and bacterial diseases.

Deficiency Diseases

A number of chemical elements are necessary for healthy plant growth and lack of them results in poor general health as well as more or less specific symptoms, usually manifested through the abnormal appearance of the leaves. It is, however, not always easy to distinguish the different deficiencies either from one another or from other causes, such as virus diseases or weather damage.

Perhaps the most common deficiency disease is calcium-induced iron deficiency or 'lime chlorosis'. This occurs on alkaline soils where the alkalinity is predominantly due to calcium rather than magnesium salts and is particularly common in 'lime-hating' plants such as camellias and members of the rhododendron family (*Ericaceae*). The typical symptoms are yellowing of the leaves between the veins with the latter remaining bright green and, if the condition persists, loss of foliage, cessation of growth and eventual death. The cure is either not to grow lime-hating plants in limey soils or the regular application of iron in a form in which the plants can take it up (e.g. Murphy's Sequestrene). The lime content of the soil can be measured indirectly by determining its 'pH' using one of the cheap soil analysis kits available in horticultural retailers. Generally if the value is greater than 6.0 you are likely to have problems with the more sensitive lime-haters.

Lime chlorosis apart, mineral deficiencies are unlikely in most rock gardens since rock plants generally have lower nutrient requirements than more vigorous growers such as vegetables or herbaceous perennials. Plants growing on very 'thin' screes, containing little soil or organic matter, or which have been growing for long periods without feeding in containers such as troughs, may suffer from nitrogen deficiency, which results in poor growth with small, pale leaves. The best way to correct this is to apply a top dressing of gritty soil with leafmould if available, and with an organic fertilizer such as hoof and horn or fish meal mixed in. This way any other nutrients in short supply are also likely to be made up to satisfactory levels. An alternative approach, which should prevent deficiencies ever developing, is to apply a general purpose fertilizer containing nitrogen along with the other nutrients required in substantial amounts (phosphorus and potassium), once or twice a year. 'Growmore' is an appropriate solid fertilizer to use while some gardeners prefer to use a liquid fertilizer such as 'Phostrogen'.

If deficiencies other than those above are suspected, for example when plants remain unhealthy or fail to grow satisfactorily even though they show no obvious signs of infestation by pests or diseases and growing conditions are satisfactory, it may be worth arranging a complete soil analysis. This can generally be obtained locally by taking or sending a representative soil sample to a horticultural or agricultural training college or Department of Agriculture and Fisheries laboratory. Formerly this was a free service but now you are likely to have to pay for the analysis. The basic analysis is usually for the three major nutrients (N:P:K) plus calcium and magnesium, but analysis for any other of the essential elements (iron, manganese, boron, copper, sulphur, molybdenum, zinc) can usually be arranged if it is thought that one of them is deficient.

While poor growth may be caused by nutrient deficiencies it should be realised that excesses of nutrients can also be damaging. This is particularly true in the case of slow-growing plants such as alpines and applies especially to ericaceous plants and others from low-nutrient habitats. These plants are simply not adapted to cope with high levels of available nutrients since they never encounter them in the wild. High levels of nitrogen can be particularly damaging and great care should be taken never to overdo applications of soluble nitrogenous fertilizers – it is much better to apply the nitrogen in slow-release organic form or as part of a balanced compound inorganic fertilizer.

The whole subject of pests and diseases in plants is excellently surveyed by Buczacki and Harris in *Collins Guide to the Pests, Diseases and Disorders of Plants*.

Rock Garden Construction

by W. K. Aslet

In making a rock garden, large or small, we are creating an illusion – i.e., trying to give the impression that the rocks are the visible outcrops of a great natural mass beneath. We do not, however, now follow the old advice to bury the rocks to such an extent that nine-tenths of their bulk is beneath the soil, like icebergs in the sea! Perfection, perhaps! But forbiddingly expensive.

Our effect is most likely to be achieved if we remember that the rocks we are likely to use occur naturally in strata, and build accordingly. There is no need to be a geologist: one need only pause and think of rocks in a quarry, or at the seaside (one of the best places to study them). One sees that they occur in layers, and it is clear that, however variably the outer portions are weather-worn and eroded, each still lies in the same relative position to the others, apart, of course, from tumbled blocks and debris lower down. The art, then, in constructing an attractive rock garden is to build it so that the rocks *look right*, using all one's ingenuity in making outcrops and recesses, valleys, cliffs, and even isolated groupings of rocks. Natural strata, as is readily seen in many cliffs, may be tilted at any angle – forwards, backwards, or up on edge.

Here practical considerations come in. It is rather dull to build rocks in a dead flat horizontal plane, though on a flat "island" site it may be best, as a backward, downward tilt into the mass on one face will obviously result in a forward, downward tilt on the opposite side – difficult to clothe with plants: all rain and other water will run down and off, instead of back among the roots. *Some* backward tilt of the strata is desirable for the latter reason, and to retain soil and prevent erosion, while it also helps stability. Erosion, too, is likely if the surfaces of the pockets or beds of soil are too steep – so get height with the rocks themselves and have the pockets comparatively level. Steeper beds can be made using a coarse scree mixture with a skeleton of "check-stones" set in just beneath the surface across the slope.

Before building, the first essential for site and soil is good drainage. Often this need be no worry at all, its difficulty being frequently exaggerated. Provided that water can move freely through the soil (largely a matter of soil texture) to the lower parts of our structure and can then escape, even if the lowest area is wet, good use can be made of this part for simulating the outflow of a stream. This may then be assumed to flow through a miniature bog garden and what could be a nicer feature to accompany our rock garden than a pool appropriately planted? There are a few choice aquatics ideal for the smallest pond, and a long list could be made of dwarf moisture-loving plants to surround it.

In the preparation of the site, attend to essential drainage and make absolutely sure that perennial weeds have been eliminated – they are difficult to get out afterwards. Consolidate carefully the area to be built on, as any subsequent sinking will be less easy to correct. Allow for an adequate depth of good soil: some, perhaps rougher, can be put on the site before building, and more – the best – can be added later to fill up the pockets. Now, shape the soil to the approximate contours required. You may have worked this out beforehand on a bed of sand with rock fragments or little wooden blocks, or even on a tea-tray with brown sugar for soil and sugar-knobs for rocks! To me, a model seems a much better guide than any sketch-plan. It cannot be accurately followed, but neither can a plan, for rocks are not regular units of precise size and shape.

Much can be done, especially on a flat site, to increase the height of one's rock-work and to save importing soil, by excavating part of the site, and using the resulting soil to build up (providing the lower area can be adequately drained). Here again, the digging of a pond will provide extra soil. If you do this, do not bury the good top soil, and remember that any exposed subsoil must be well covered with a good planting medium.

I never build rockwork like a wall, or a house, by putting in a foundation and building the whole of the lowest layer. With a spade I chop out a bed for the base of a rock in its selected position, at the angle at which I think it will "sit right," manoeuvre it up there with a truck or plank, finally adjusting it with a crowbar and if necessary small stones for wedging. When finally satisfied I ram the soil beneath and behind it very firmly to ensure stability.

I like to start thus by selecting one of my biggest lumps of rock and setting it up as the "nose" of the most prominent outcrop. I

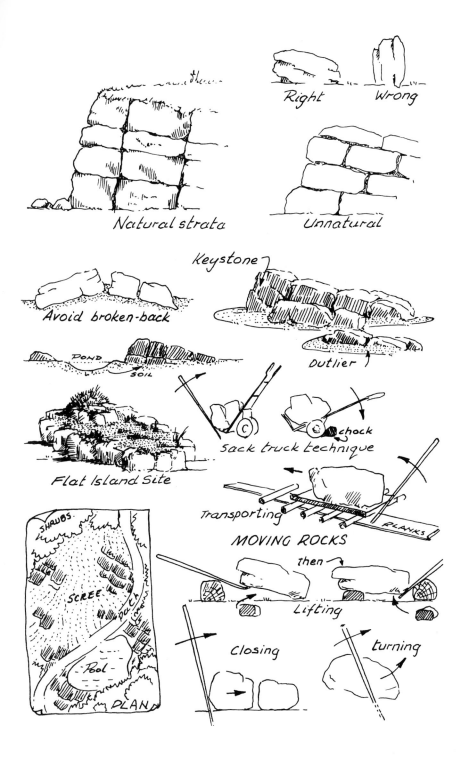

Natural strata

Right   Wrong

Unnatural

Keystone

Avoid broken-back

Outlier

POND

SOIL

Flat Island Site

Sack truck technique   chock

Transporting   PLANKS

MOVING ROCKS

then

Lifting

SHRUBS

SCREE

Pool

PLAN

Closing   turning

call this my "Keystone." I stalk around it, considering all its angles and their implications. Much time and thought are given to this, as it sets the angles of "tip" for all the strata, and all the other main outcrops and any valleys, etc., must "run with it." All other rocks, even isolated "out-liers" a long way off in turf, will be set in relation to it. Sometimes a side view of strata will be preferable to a head-on aspect. From my "keystone" I build back, and out, and even down, and away in all directions, setting up secondary "keystones" as the "noses" of other main features, again using the larger rocks. The angles of tip are very important and a *gentle* inclination is usually the most practical, as with steep angles it becomes difficult to "return" the strata into the soil, especially when making both sides of a valley. I like to keep the natural effect by using the most weathered rocks near the top and in outlying parts. Rules, however, are made to be broken and a thin stone can often be used on edge to obtain height with less bulk, thus giving more planting space behind it. Judge each stone on whether it looks right to you. A lot of economy can be exercised by using the biggest pieces for the prominent "noses" and fading them back into the earth with progressively smaller rocks. Inevitably, later on one is left with a number of rejected, awkward pieces. One has to "lose" them at the back or sides, and often they look better if more deeply buried. At this stage, too, one makes some unsatisfactory joints that look ugly. There is no need to worry about these. They are easily "planted out" by a judiciously placed small shrub or dwarf conifer. Crevices can be packed with turf fibre or stringy peat to retain soil and it is often well worth planting these cracks as you build, as at no other time can you get foot-long roots back at full stretch to help the plants through the next dry spring. When you've finished, brush the rocks clean and wash them off. Bad scratches can be "touched up" with soot-water, and if the rocks look raw they can be weathered by spraying with a liquid manure. For steps and paved paths use stone that is a reasonable match, likewise with any chippings for screes or surfacing.

Streams, waterfalls and stone bridges should, like ponds, be very strongly made and no cement should show. Recessed or "brushed-out" joints are much more natural than "flush" pointing. Cement, if used, is easily coloured to blend with rock.

Drifts of turf may run up between groups of rock and can make the whole thing look bigger. Never run turf down into water! And do always remember the factor of maintenance, and have any grass shaped for easy mowing. Areas of dwarf heathers can also separate or surround groups of rocks, or extend the background and make the whole thing look larger while economising in stone. The illusion of rock outcropping can be created by using very little rock indeed, so a little piece of mountain scenery and some scree beds for choice plants need not cost much.

The position of our rock garden should be open and reasonably sunny; it must not be under trees because of drip and falling leaves. Provision for shade plants can be made alongside rocks and shrubs, and in the valleys. Our background can be planted with suitable small shrubs.

Handling the stone. Pieces of up to 2 cwt. (quite large enough for the ordinary garden), are easily carted about on a sack truck with pneumatic tyres, which will go readily over quite soft ground. They are also very easily moved about with planks and rollers, or even by placing them on a plank and tilting it, letting them slide down. For smaller stones a good wheelbarrow is all that is needed. It is not necessary to lift heavy stones; they are easy to raise on to blocks (for picking up on a truck or plank) by means of a good iron crowbar. This is also essential for final adjustments, like raising the rock sufficiently to chock it up or to get the tilt correct. A heavy hammer and cold chisel can be useful to remove awkward corners, especially when laying paving. Ramming all stones tightly is essential, and wooden rammers are best. Ash tool handles of various sizes are ideal. Now for some notes on various types of rock.

Sandstone. e.g. Sussex. Excellent; porous; plants like it. Kentish Rag. Hard and heavy, but good. Old Red. Not so good, Very hard and angular if freshly quarried.

Limestone. Westmorland. Hard, heavy. The most popular. Easy to lay. Goes very white in town air. Too much of it is used. Try a change!

Cotswold. Lovely! Also good for chippings.

Dorset. Excellent, especially if weathered rock can be obtained.

Granite. Hard, angular, ugly.

Tufa. Porous and light. Plants love it and so do I, but so also do weeds!

If a good local stone is available it is often best, and always cheapest. Order pieces as large as you feel you can handle; if a lot of small bits are used they may well be lost sight of under your plants.

Finally the soil; any good mixture, such as potting soil with a lot of extra chippings for drainage, is suitable. Special areas may be made up for particular plants, e.g. for Ericaceæ, Asiatic Gentians, scree plants, etc. Remember that lime will travel down in soil water but not up, so prepare higher parts for lime haters if they are to be grown as well as plants that need lime. Very few need it, but the majority of rock garden plants will tolerate it.

For further reading:–
   Natural Rock Gardening. B. H. B. Symons-Jeune. Country Life. (The only book entirely devoted to rock garden construction.)

Alpines Without a Rock Garden

by David Mowle

Right from the moment of its foundation our Society has distanced itself from the art of building rock gardens. Not only is the disposition of the rock in an artistic way difficult but the resultant work rarely blends into our largely lowland living areas and has nothing directly to do with growing plants. We have been free as a Society therefore to experiment with the many ways in which alpine plants can be fitted into a garden plan. Even the smallest garden encompasses a range of growing conditions, from sunshine to shade, from draughty to sheltered, and perhaps from quick drying to more permanently moist. There are alpine plants to clothe all these sites and great fun to be had, together with inevitable disappointments, in matching the plants to the site.

Let us begin with the existing soil in a level garden. The alpine plants we will be able to grow still require the normal rules of good cultivation to be followed. If stagnant water tends to accumulate an escape route for it must be provided. Heavy clay and light sand both require organic matter to be added until a good fertile soil has been achieved. Artificial fertilizers will not be required.

If the garden has areas of open shade on the north side of a building or fence a wide range of plants from the high woodlands of the world will grow there. The light shade from small trees is suitable but the heavier shade and drier conditions under forest trees will restrict the choice. Trilliums and hellebores, erythroniums and *Cyclamen hederifolium* and *C. coum* will provide a basic planting and *Anemone nemorosa* and *A. apennina*, corydalis and *Primula polyneura* and *P. geraniifolia* will gently colonize such areas. Dryness is the enemy of these plants so in the drier areas of the country additional organic matter worked into the soil or top dressing with peat will be appreciated.

Where the light shade comes from deciduous trees the site will be warmed by the early spring sunshine and Snowdrops and

Crocus will start the display. A planting of *Crocus nudiflorus* will end the season, too, with its lilac goblets opening in October.

A different range of plants can be grown as we move out of the shade into the sunnier garden. On the sunnier side of small trees the soil will tend to dry out in the summer and here a wide range of alpine bulbs will thrive. Crocuses again of course but also dwarf narcissi, scillas, chionodoxas and some fritillaries, notably *FF. pyrenaica, involucrata* and *pallidiflora*. In positions which retain slightly more moisture in the summer named forms of *Phlox douglasii* and *P. subulata* will form mats of different colours in late spring to be followed by *Campanula carpatica, Gentiana septemfida* and *G. lagodechiana*. When considering suitable plants for these open, level sites the appearance of the bed in winter assumes importance and requires a framework of evergreen subjects of contrasting or complementary colours, shapes and textures. Dwarf conifers are available in wide variety (see p. 99), along with dwarf Hollies, golden Box and dwarf cotoneasters. The autumn flowering shrub *Saturea subspicata*, although not evergreen, will attract the late flying butterflies to its 30cm high flower spikes.

The raised bed

The list of plants we have been considering for a level bed of existing (if well nourished) soil has included hardly any of the very dwarf, high mountain plants. If tried in these conditions they will give some satisfaction for a year or perhaps two but will then fade away rather than grow and thrive. The reasons for this are probably complex but success can be achieved by providing a 20cm deep layer of very gritty soil in which the plants grow. This grittiness is to allow rain water to drain very quickly from the plants' roots; but do not confuse good drainage with dryness. Moisture must be present in plenty during the growing season.

The easiest way to ensure good drainage of water from the alpine bed is to raise the level above that of the surrounding soil. Slopes can be terraced using retaining walls whose height will depend on the slope of the ground. On level ground the retaining walls will need to surround the bed but need be no more than 20cm in height. The walls must allow rainwater to run out freely so dry-stone walling is ideal and any pointing between bricks or reconstituted blocks must leave frequent drainage passages. It is usual to sink the bottom course of stonework 2–5cm below ground

10. *Galanthus ikariae*

11. *Erythronium* 'White Beauty'

12. *Narcissus* 'Jack Snipe'

level to ensure stability of the wall, and also to slope the wall gently back into the bed. Each succeeding layer of building blocks must be placed across the joints of the layer beneath and each stone must sit firmly in place. It is useful to fix a string in position to indicate the top level of the wall and to build up to it but an absolutely straight upper edge is not necessarily appropriate as plants will be encouraged to grow over the edge of the mature bed.

The building material used for these low retaining walls should be selected carefully to fit the garden setting. Sandstones and limestones can be beautiful in themselves but often look out of place in a brickbuilt suburban environment. Brickbuilt low walls have a neatness which can mirror the neatness of alpine plants. In a woodland environment log walls look entirely appropriate and are thoroughly satisfactory. Not only are locally available materials likely to be appropriate but, as transport makes up so large a part of the cost, more economical as well.

The more regular the building blocks are the easier it is to construct a stable wall but the more difficult to be sure that rain water can run from the soil behind. The minimum of pointing between the layers should be used – preferably none at all – so that the free drainage of water from the soil mixture can be guaranteed.

When the wall is finally built check once again that it is all stable and strong enough to support the soil mixture behind it.

The condition of the ground below the new bed is not as critical as was once thought. It should be a normal garden soil, lightly dug over, and free of all perennial weeds. The mix to fill the bed would typically be made from one part of garden soil, one part of stone chippings and one part of peat, leafmould or other vegetable fibre. In this free draining, humusy mix a very large variety of alpine plants will thrive. Having stated the basic ratio of the mix let us examine each component in turn.

If the soil of the garden tends towards clay then larger volumes of chippings and peat will be required to make a satisfactory mixture. A soil rich in humus will obviously need less organic matter to be added. Sandy soils need more care, however. Unless the sand particles are large, with many of them at least 1–2mm across, the flow of air through the mix will not be as free as that promoted by gravel or stone chippings with an average size of 6–10mm. It is best therefore to ignore any fine sand in calculating the amount of chippings required as it is very unlikely that you will incorporate too large a proportion of the latter.

The chippings must be chosen to complement the stone used in the low walls and are also best bought locally to limit cost. Using the recommended 1:1:1 mixture one tonne of chippings would make a bed the required 20cm deep and some 20 square metres in area, leaving a few over to top-dress the bed after planting. Don't try to economise by using fewer chippings than one third of the mix. It is at about this proportion with an average loam soil that the nature of the mixture changes so that it becomes loose and well aerated as well as quick draining and resistant to compaction however firmly it is trodden on.

The vegetable fibre constituent of the mix helps to retain vital moisture and reduces the tendency of soil particles to wash down gradually to the bottom of the bed. Peat, leafmould, composted forest bark or the contents of a *good* compost heap are all suitable additives and rather more than one third would be useful in a garden in low rainfall areas.

Filling the bed

After lightly forking the ground beneath the bed spread a layer of the mix some 15cm deep over it and tread it down. Tread it particularly well immediately behind the enclosing wall to aid stability. Carry on filling the bed in layers in this way until the soil level is about 2cm below the top of the wall.

Having got this far you have earned a rest! Sit down a short distance from the bed and try to decide whether you will be able to reach into the centre of it for the inevitable weeding and to tend your plants. If not, now is the time to place a few stepping stones at suitable spots over the bed. These will need to be slightly above the present soil level to allow for the 2cm depth of top dressing and for the slight settling that will inevitably take place. When placing the stones, tread heavily round them to try to reduce this settlement to a minimum.

Because of settlement it is very difficult to build a satisfactory bed deeper than 60cm (2'). The treading down will need to be very heavy and it is best to leave the filling for a few weeks before adding the top 15cm of mixture. If it rains during this settlement period, so much the better.

If slightly higher walls are being attempted they can be made very attractive by planting suitable alpines through the wall as building and filling proceeds. For the sunny side of the wall sun-lovers like thymes, sempervivums and aubrieta are suitable while the shady side will provide a home for ramondas, haberleas and various primulas, such as *Primula rubra, P. marginata* and the *P. x pubescens* hybrids. The plants should be placed at the bottoms of the vertical crevices between the stones and jammed in very firmly using small wedges of the material of the wall or they will wash out. The plants must have sufficient root growth to stretch well back into the soil mix behind the wall. The soil mix itself must be of course really firmly trodden or settlement may tear the roots of the plants from their crowns, with fatal results.

Returning to the top of the new bed, planting can now begin, although any time left for settlement will be rewarded by stability later. When planting, first place those larger plants chosen to give winter shape. If the bed has some changes of level it is usually considered more satisfactory to place the low, spreading plants at the highest points and the tall slender plants at the lowest points. Secondly, it is best to group these architectural plants together rather than spread them evenly over the surface. When the positions are chosen tease out the roots of the plants, make a hole larger than seems necessary and spread the roots out well in it. Adjust the height of the plant so that it will look right after vigorous firming in and the addition of a top dressing of chippings. If, on reflection, it does not look right, lever it up gently with a garden fork and begin again! Remember, you will be looking at this bed for ten years or more so you must get it right. In any case, the gritty alpine soil will fall away from the roots quite easily even after firm treading so that no harm is done in lifting and resetting. Finally, give the plants a generous watering.

Having planted a framework of larger plants the time has come to plant the smaller alpines. You cannot be so cavalier in digging these up for a second attempt so greater care is needed in getting the depth of planting correct, but at least you will have had some practice! The roots of the smaller plants will be in the soil mixture but try to arrange for the crowns of the plants to be just clear of the soil and sitting in the 2cm layer of pure chippings with which you are top dressing the bed. Don't forget to include some bulbs in your planting. Most of them prefer to be planted about 7–10cm down. If they are in growth in a pot at the time of planting try to avoid disturbing the root-ball as the roots of many bulbs are sensitive to disturbance: just plant the whole potful. The root-balls of non-bulbous plants must, on the other hand, always be teased out on planting to ensure intimate contact with the soil in the bed.

The question of how to identify your plants has never been satis-factorily resolved. Most labels detract from the appearance of the planting and blackbirds love pulling them out. Black labels with white-writing (or scratchings) suffer least from these two dis-advantages. If the bed is not too large why not draw a plan showing the plant names? This method has the advantage of reminding you five years later which plants did not survive and start you trying to decide why. Remember that each plant prefers not only a satisfactory soil mixture, which you have provided, but also a certain balance between sunlight intensity, moisture supply and moisture removal. Thus a Kabschia saxifrage can be burnt in a hot summer in one site, yet only a few metres away, where it receives shade at mid-day from a dwarf conifer or a rock, can flourish.

The scree bed

The raised bed just described will grow a very wide range of alpine plants to perfection but there are just a few – those coming from the more extreme high alpine situations – which require even better drainage than is supplied by the recommended mixture. The growing mixture for the more temperamental high alpines should therefore be almost all stone chippings with the admixture of, at most, one fifth of leaf-soil or peat. The raised scree bed can be built in the same manner as was recommended for the raised bed but there appears to be no unanimity on the preferred depth. The reason for this is that here we are not looking at a new concept for growing alpine plants but merely at a refinement for growing the most difficult. Many of the plants grown will be small and in culti-vation will not form the extensive root growth reported from the wild. It seems sensible, therefore, to specify the same minimum depth of scree mixture as was recommended for the normal raised bed, namely 20cm, and the writer has a scree to this specification which has given pleasure over ten years.

The 20cm layer consists of 6mm granite chippings mixed with about one fifth of their volume of moss peat which is spread on top of the normal fertile garden soil. A slight slope of the ground is enough to give normal drainage under the very sharply drained scree layer. With this arrangement it has proved possible to blend the scree into the general garden scene by planting dwarf conifers which obtain their nourishment from the soil beneath the scree. European androsaces grow in this scree and *Campanula alpestris* hangs its huge bells just above the chippings each year. A deeper scree nearby, with just over 30cm depth of chippings and slightly higher surrounding walls was made from one fifth of garden soil mixed with the 6mm chippings. Plants have taken longer to establish themselves in this mix but have formed compact floriferous mats.

When planting out from pots into a scree mix all the soil should be removed from the roots of the plant and great care taken to spread them out among the unstable chippings. Watering will be essential for a few weeks after planting if rain is absent but after becoming established scree plants seem less affected by drought conditions than plants in a normal raised bed. Annual feeding of a scree is advisable and bone-meal has long been recommended for this job, perhaps with the addition of one sixth part of potassium sulphate. The more modern equivalent is a slow-release fertilizer with approximately equal proportions of nitrogen, phosphorus and potassium.

The peat bed

The use of scree beds to grow alpine plants has a written history of over a century but the use of peat beds was first recorded only just over fifty years ago. Its aim is to provide good growing conditions for those plants which seek out in nature a moist, spongy, often acidic soil such as is found in mature woodland or on a moist moorland. In the peat bed dwarf rhododendrons and cassiopes from the high moorlands of the Himalayas can grow next to the North American trilliums, the shortias of Japan and the otherwise difficult Petiolarid primulas.

If the natural soil of a garden contains lime it is unlikely that a peat bed will prove satisfactory. For the gardener who insists on growing peat-loving plants in a lime rich area a trough filled with a peaty soil mixture is likely to give more permanent pleasure than a peat bed, though even then rainwater or other lime-free water will have to be used for watering.

The short history of the peat bed has developed out of using peat blocks instead of walling stone to support low terraces of peat-enriched soil. The continual supply of moisture required in this type of habitat is not so easily arranged in free-standing beds though this would be possible in areas of higher rainfall.

The need to maintain a high moisture level in the bed will dictate its position and aspect: north sloping and perhaps lightly shaded in drier areas but receiving more direct sunlight in cooler and moister gardens. The peat blocks of the terrace steps must always be moist and so it is not advisable to build to any great height. Thirty centimetres high is a sensible maximum, otherwise the top front corners will dry out rapidly. The aim is to encourage dwarf ericaceous plants to clothe the peat blocks to create a living wall and this must be arranged before the blocks have begun to weather away. Gaultherias such as *GG. adenothrix, cuneata, miqueliana* and *nummularioides* are ideal creeping shrubs for this use.

The peat blocks themselves are not always easy to procure. For those within travelling distance of a commercial peat cutting area, blocks the ideal 30cm cube can be obtained but if necessary the thin blocks offered as fuel will suffice. These will require several days totally immersed in water before they will be wet enough to use. If all else fails the walls can be built of stone, though the charm of the planted peat walls will be lost.

The soil of the terraces still needs to be well drained and weed-free and in attending to this the levels can be adjusted so that the garden soil stops 10cm below the final terrace level. A top layer should then be mixed from three parts coarse moss peat (not granulated), one part of lime-free 4mm chippings or coarse sand and one part of the local (lime-free) soil. These proportions are by no means critical but are offered as a general indication of a satisfactory mix. Fresh top dressings of peat will be part of the routine maintenance of the bed.

This top layer rich in peat needs to remain fairly loose so after spreading it over the area, one treading down is all that is required. Access for weeding without the need to tread on the bed is essential and stepping stones or upended blocks of durable wood will have to be suitably arranged.

Trough gardens

The size of the beds so far described could range from one to many square metres, but similar soil mixtures filled into old stone troughs have proved to be ideal for cultivating the very tiniest alpine plants. It is very rare nowadays to find an old stone trough standing empty at a reasonable asking price but a suitable alternative can be made quite cheaply.

Concrete must weather for a very long time before plants find it sympathetic but by using peat in addition to cement and sand a trough can be made which the plants will love. The addition of peat weakens the trough mechanically so a wire mesh reinforcement or similar will be needed. Details of how to make such a trough have been given in the next chapter.

Home-made Troughs

by Sid Lilley and John Good

All of us admire the genuine old stone troughs and sinks over-flowing with choice alpines to be found in many an enthusiast's garden and yearn for a collection of our own. Alas, like all antiques they get ever scarcer and more expensive and so are, for most of us, to all intents and purposes unobtainable. We must either forget the idea of trough and sink gardening or seek alterna-tives to the genuine articles.

One possibility is a new stone trough; one which has been made from a block of stone specifically for the purpose of providing a home for plants. Such are not readily available but can be found in some specialist alpine nurseries or, more likely, at Chelsea or one of the larger provincial flower shows. The best will have been made from old blocks of stone which are already well weathered but they are likely to be expensive. Those cut from newly quarried stone will generally be cheaper and may well be acceptable, par-ticularly in the garden of a new house where they may indeed look more appropriate. As an alternative to purchase you could make one yourself, or commission someone handy to do the job for you.

First find your block of stone, which should be of suitable size and shape and free from fractures or obvious lines of weakness. Avoid kinds of rock which are known to be prone to crumbling, flaking or splitting – hard sandstone and millstone grit are prob-ably the best widely available materials. The tools you will need are a heavy duty angle grinder with a masonry cutting disc of the type used by roadmen to cut paving slabs and a heavy duty electric hammer drill with an assortment of bits. Both these items can be hired from any reasonable tool hire company.

Choosing a place where you can work without interruption and where flying stone chips will not be an unacceptable hazard, set your block of stone up firmly, so that it will not rock or tilt when under attack. Decide on what thickness you want the walls of the trough to be, bearing in mind that old troughs generally have thick walls but that this reduces the number of plants that can be grown. Less than 50mm would probably be inadvisable anyway on grounds of strength. Next, mark out the inside dimensions of the trough with an old chisel or screwdriver held against a straight edge. Now, having donned protective clothing including a breathing mask and goggles, cut out to the depth required all round with the cutting disc, making sure to leave a thickness of at least 50mm at the base. A series of criss-cross cuts should now be made to the same depth, resulting in a pattern of diamonds within the area to be removed. Using the hammer drill, experiment with different bits until you find one that suits you best and then chip and gouge out the stone diamonds, finally cleaning up the base and sides. Rounding off the inner top edge of the trough will disguise the severe lines of the cutting disc. If it seems appropriate to do so you can produce the equivalents of the marks made by the cutting tools of some long-dead stone mason and the chips and gouges produced by a century in the farmyard or kitchen, but do not overdo it. The final act, using a straightforward 20–30mm diameter masonry bit, is to drill a number of drainage holes in the base.

Another much more straightforward way of making a stone 'trough', quite different in conception from that hollowed out from the block, is to build one. In this case walls of suitable thinly bedded stone, such as Cotswold limestone, slate or shale are built on a base of the same material or some acceptable substitute such as a paving slab. The base can be of any shape. Before you start make sure that you have an ample supply of stone to hand for the job since even the smallest wall swallows up a surprisingly large amount. The wall is built up with mortar in the normal way, small holes being left at intervals around the base to provide drainage. What you will end up with is really a miniature enclosed raised bed rather than a trough but we have seen some extremely attractive ones.

Another alternative, often seen in areas where stone which is easily cleft such as slate is available, is the slab or box trough. Of course, a whole range of artificial materials could be used instead. I have seen V-shaped ones made from two slates, one let into a rebate in the other at the bottom and the two held together by rods at each end near the top, the ends being tightly fitting triangles of slate. Commoner, however, is the box made from five pieces of slate – two sides, two ends and a base, the whole being held together by threaded steel tie-rods passed through holes in the slates and secured with nuts. This sounds ugly, but if the tie rods, which could be made to order in any small engineering workshop, are of just the right length, and the holes are countersunk on the outside to take the nut, this need not be so. These troughs have the advantage of being very light in weight and are easily dismantled so that they are ideal for someone who has to move house often or who likes frequently to rearrange his (or more likely her) garden.

All of the containers described so far have been made from stone; the remainder of this article is concerned with counterfeiting. Hypertufa was a name coined by an early president of our Society, F. H. Fisher, for a tufa rock substitute made by incorporating peat into a mortar mix. The purpose of the peat, which *must* be very fine and dry, is to make the mortar porous and to give it a more natural texture and tone than concrete. In Fisher's formula the three constituents; sand, cement and Sorbex peat were mixed in the ratios 1:1:2 (by bulk *not* weight). To my (J. G.) knowledge Sorbex peat is no longer available, and as I have not seen it I cannot tell whether it had some special properties, but I have found dry sphagnum peat rubbed through an eighth inch (2.5mm) sieve perfectly suitable. Increasing the proportion of sand in the mix will, naturally, give the finished article an appearance more nearly resembling sandstone than tufa while increasing the cement will make it look more like limestone, at the same time increasing its weight.

Hypertufa can be used both to make troughs or to disguise glazed sinks or other trough-shaped items to which it can be induced to stick. Taking the hypertufa trough first: one must acquire or make a suitable mould. The simplest consists of no more than two stout cardboard boxes, one fitting inside the other and leaving a sufficiently wide gap to form the walls of the trough. An alternative is a wooden mould which can be constructed in such a way that when the trough is dry it can be removed without damaging the latter and used again. However, the cardboard boxes have the advantages of simplicity and of producing a trough of slightly irregular, less angular shape, which looks more natural. Yet another alternative mould is a hole in the ground of suitable size and shape into which an inner mould is placed. It should be borne in mind that a trough cast in this way will take a long time to dry and will have to be excavated and lifted when it is ready.

Returning to the cardboard box mould as being the most com-

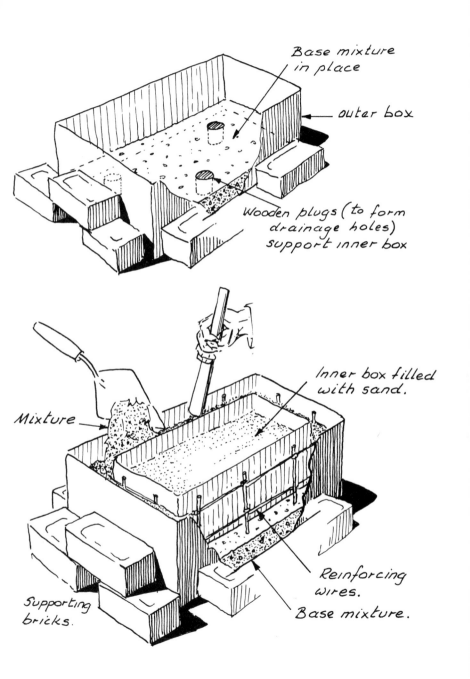

Base mixture in place

outer box

Wooden plugs (to form drainage holes) support inner box

Mixture

Inner box filled with sand.

Supporting bricks.

Reinforcing wires.

Base mixture.

monly used, the procedure is as follows. Set up the outer box on a
flat surface in a position where one can move around it freely and
where the trough can be left to dry without risk of damage for a
week or more. Next place some reinforcing material such as wire
netting or galvanized steel mesh into the base, bending it up round
the corners which are the most vulnerable part of the finished
trough. Have ready four pieces of broom handle or similar about
25–50mm long (the depth of the base of the trough). Finally place
some bricks or concrete blocks around the outside of the box to
give it support.

Now mix the hypertufa dry and then add sufficient water to give
a thick, creamy consistency. If desired some PVA bonding agent,
such as 'Unibond', can be added to the mix, diluted as directed for
eliminating flaking and dusting of concrete floors. This will help to
strengthen the trough and make it more resistant to weather
damage. It will also make it less porous, which may be considered
disadvantageous for the plants that will grow in it, although I have
no evidence that this is so. Pour sufficient of the mix into the box
to give the depth required for the trough base and while it is still
wet press the four pieces of broom handle into it, one near each
corner. These will provide a firm platform for the inner box while
the trough is being made and, when removed, will leave the
essential drainage holes.

Next place the inner cardboard box and support its walls from
inside with any suitable material – expanded polystyrene foam of
the type now so widely used in packaging consumer durables is
good. Pour the hypertufa into the space between the boxes,
tamping it down with a suitable piece of wood as you go to remove
air bubbles. Reinforcing material can be put in place as you go
along, using right-angle bends to strengthen the corners. When the
space between the boxes is filled to the desired height give a final
tamp down all round and then leave the trough to set.

After a day or two it should be dry enough to remove the outer
box from the sides without damage but still sufficiently soft to
enable the smooth surface to be 'roughed up', so as to disguise its
artificiality. Using an old chisel, a file and a soft brush a passable
imitation of the stone mason's work, softened by time, can be
achieved. Do not forget at this stage to tear off the inner box a
little way down so that the top inner edge of the trough can be
rounded off too.

Now leave the trough for at least another week to harden before removing the rest of the inner box and, finally, the base of the outer box and the wooden plugs. Once the new trough is set up in its chosen position it can be prematurely aged to some extent by painting it with a witches brew of nitrogen-rich material such as sour milk, urine, and water in which dung has been soaked, which will encourage the growth of mosses and liverworts.

Where it is desired to cover an old glazed sink or other receptacle with hypertufa the procedure is as follows. First remove any extraneous accoutrements – waste pipes, plughole liners etc. Next, if the surface is smooth, rough it up to provide a key for the hypertufa. In the case of a glazed sink this can be done either by chipping at the glaze with a club hammer and cold chisel – very tedious and rather dangerous – or by drilling shallow holes at regular intervals with a tile-cutting bit in a power drill.

Now mix up some PVA adhesive at the strength recommended for bonding mortar to glazed surfaces, e.g. tiles, and paint this all over the outer surface, the top edge, and for 10cm down the inside. While this is drying mix your hypertufa as already described but add much less water to give a mixture which will stick to the sides of the trough rather than sliding off. Again, PVA added to the mix will strengthen the hypertufa but in this case it will also serve to bind it very strongly to the receptacle. I find that it is easiest to do most of the application of hypertufa with the hands (protected with thin rubber gloves) rather than with a trowel and that this gives a more rounded, natural look, especially to the corners which should receive a slightly thicker layer than the remainder to allow for the greater wear and tear that they will inevitably have to endure. Make sure to take the hypertufa well down over the inner top edge of the sink and also under the outer bottom edge so that no sign of its real identity remains in view. Leave the completed imposter to partially dry before 'roughing up' as described for cast troughs.

Finally, I (J. G.) recall seeing an excellent collection of very natural-looking troughs of all sizes and various shapes in a Scottish garden which were made by a charming lady who admitted to being well past the first flush of youth. She explained how she had made them very easily *in situ* by applying hypertufa with the hands to a previously formed 'basket' of galvanized chicken mesh. No doubt there are many other equally easy and effective ways of making troughs and sinks which will delight the eye while providing a happy home for the choicest of alpines.

Cushions

by Stan Taylor

To many alpine gardeners, especially those who show their plants at the Society's shows, the cushion plant epitomizes the perfect alpine plant. A perfectly symmetrical dome covered in flowers can send such enthusiasts into raptures of delight.

So, what is it that causes so much admiration and leads visitors to the shows to declare, "they must be made of plastic", and to poke them with their fingers to find out!

Cushion plants have, in the main, developed their particular style of growth so as to be able to survive in a habitat which is hostile to plants of 'normal' size and form. In a typical alpine terrain, above the tree line, the habitat is very hostile to plant growth. Screes, moraines and rock faces are subjected to wide temperature differentials while being open to high winds, driving rain and heavy falls of snow. Any plant growing in these conditions obviously has to be specially adapted to survive. It needs to be able to avoid the damaging effects of wind and for this the dome-shaped cushion is ideal. It must be able not only to conserve moisture in times of drought, but also to shed excess – the cushion habit is ideally shaped to do this. In withstanding heavy falls of snow without damage the domed shape is, once again, ideal. We need to bear these facts in mind and to consider how they may create problems when attempting to grow high altitude cushions in cultivation.

While many high altitude plants are cushions, by no means all cushions come from the high mountains. Wherever dessication is a major environmental factor, and particularly where high winds are a common feature, cushion plants may be found. Thrift (*Armeria maritima*), Sea Campion (*Silene vulgaris* ssp. *maritima*) and the common Wall Pepper (*Sedum acre*) are examples from the British flora.

Returning to the high alpine cushions: how are we to grow these plants that seem to need such hostile conditions. We cannot hope to re-create the environment from which they come and we certainly cannot reproduce the effects of altitude. The growing, flowering and resting periods are much more clearly defined at altitude, not erratic and prolonged as they are in our gardens. As those who have visited high mountains will know, the air is very rarely still there, as it often is in the lowlands. Excess moisture, of which there can be plenty, is soon dried off by the wind, while the steeply sloping ground takes away excess water from the roots. Furthermore, the whole host of pests and diseases which afflict our plants in the gardens are much less common and aggressive in the alpine heights. Aphids, for example, are almost entirely absent at high altitudes so that the plants which grow there have had no need to develop resistance to them. Hence the extreme sensitivity of many choice cushion plants to these and other pests. However, all is not 'doom and gloom', as a visit to an AGS Show will prove. We may have aphids and Red Spider, but few of us have problems with Chamois or Ibex nibbling our rarities, and most of our gardens are free from avalanches and rock falls, so it is not a completely one-sided fight.

Having seen how cushion plants are adapted to survive in the wild, we need to emulate at least some of their basic requirements if we are to be successful with them in cultivation. I shall describe three methods of cultivation, all of which have proved successful, and are used by many leading growers.

Rock gardens, raised beds and troughs

I have grouped these three types of cultivation together because one would expect the same environmental features to apply to all of them. Most gardens have the space to create at least one of these features, enabling the gardener to grow some of the easier cushion plants. The normal rules for successful rock gardening, spelt out elsewhere in this Handbook, apply with special force to cushions. In particular it is vital that the drainage be faultless, while the presence of a layer at least 1cm thick of chippings or gravel around the collar of the plants will help prevent rot. An alternative is to plant them in rockwork such that all surface moisture drains away.

Many cushion plants can be cultivated in the open ground if these fundamental precautions are taken, indeed there are few that cannot, although some require overhead protection with a cloche or a pane of glass through the winter. One group which is commonly grown and among which are some of the finest cushion plants, are the saxifrages. Many of the smaller members of the silver section of the genus form cushions but it is the Kabschia section which provides the gems. They are most accommodating plants and so long as they are never allowed to dry out at the root during their growing period they will reward you with complete domes of flower every year. The range of saxifrages available, including hybrids, is over six hundred, in colours ranging from white through every shade of pink and yellow to scarlet, and when not in flower the cushions are most attractive.

One of the most successful ways to grow saxifrages, as well as many other choice cushion plants, is on Tufa rock (see page 81). Small plants should be selected for planting into holes which are easily made in the soft porous rock with an old chisel or large screwdriver. A little John Innes No. 2 compost or similar is filtered in around the roots and the tufa removed when making the hole is put back around the collar of the plant, which is then watered thoroughly with a can equipped with a fine rose. The plants must be kept moist at all times until established – throughout the first summer in the case of spring planting.

A list of some other plants which may be grown outside will be found at the end of this article.

Cold frames and raised plunge frames

By using a cold frame or plunge bed we can increase quite considerably the range of cushion plants we can grow. The main reason for this is that we can control the growing environment to some extent. By growing plants in pots we can vary the growing medium. By rotating the pots on a regular basis we can ensure even growth and better shaped cushions while more even flowering will also be achieved. More importantly, we can control the amount of water the plants receive, which is not possible in the open ground. This is of crucial significance in the case of those cushion plants which demand a reduction in soil water content as dormancy approaches.

The conventional cold frame, with wooden, sloping sides has two major drawbacks in comparison with a plunge bed such as that shown opposite. Light and ventilation are both restricted, so

13. Plunge frame in summer

14. Saxifrages in tufa

15. *Dionysia lamingtonii*

that plants grown around the edges of the cold frame will get drawn because of lack of light, while during wet weather from October to December, when the plants need overhead protection, ventilation is restricted. Glass sided cold frames are better for light access but ventilation is still a problem.

I would advocate the use of clay pots, plunged to their rims, for growing plants in all types of frames unless, in the case of a cold frame, the pots are to be free standing, in which case plastic pots are probably better. Plunge material is a matter of personal choice and local availability and cost but I use washed builders' sand. Kept moist, it does not collapse when pots are removed, which sometimes occurs with pea gravel and peat mixtures. Washed sand is porous enough not to become waterlogged and retains sufficient moisture to keep the plunged pots just right during the dormant months.

The plunge frame should be deep enough to take a twelve inch (30cm) pot with space beneath for drainage. The tops of the pots should be level with the top of the frame. The covers need to be about 45cm above the top of the frame, allowing ventilation from the sides by louvres or sliding glass panels. The side ventilation, as hinted above, is most important, allowing a passage of air over the plants and thus reducing the risk of fungal diseases which often kill otherwise healthy plants as they are going into dormancy. The covers should be removed as soon as possible in spring, normally about April in Britain, and returned when dank conditions and falling temperatures suggest that they are needed (about November).

The potting compost used is again a matter of personal choice and is dependent to a large extent on the amount of time one can devote to watering. However, the following points should be borne in mind. Most cushion plants grow on rock faces and screes so need perfect drainage. The cushions must be kept 'in character' so the compost needs to be lean, perhaps three parts John Innes No. 2 to two parts sharp grit for lime tolerant plants, three parts lime-free leafmould to two parts grit for lime haters. Cushion plants grown in such composts should never be allowed to dry out during the summer or scorching of the cushions will occur, badly disfiguring the plant.

Listed at the end of this article is a range of cushion plants suitable for growing in frames, but all the plants suggested for the open ground may, of course, also be grown in this way.

The alpine house

Growing good cushion plants in the alpine house, far from solving all the problems, presents some special ones. Alpine houses in summer became hot and dry, not a good environment for most of the cushion plants. Ensuring sufficient ventilation is always a problem, along with that of providing adequate shading. Too much shade and the cushions become drawn, too little and the temperature rises with the inevitable risk of scorching. Meticulous attention to watering in these conditions is essential. Pots should again be plunged if possible, to alleviate the problem of plants drying out at the root. Potting composts should, if anything, be 'leaner' than those used for cushions grown outside in the plunge frame, adding an additional part of grit. This will help to combat the effects of being grown under glass.

There are, however, some plants which appear to prefer alpine house conditions and amongst these are the dionysias. They mainly come from hot arid areas (Afghanistan and Iran), where summer temperatures are very high and humidity is very low. Unfortunately they are not easy plants to grow and could not be recommended to the real beginner, but a challenge is half the fun in gardening as in other aspects of life so a list of some of the easier species is included in the Appendix.

To sum up: to grow good cushion plants the following six points need to be observed:

(a) ensure good drainage
(b) plants must not be allowed to dry out at the root during the growing season
(c) ensure maximum ventilation at all times
(d) keep compost as 'lean' as possible
(e) ensure good all round access to light
(f) turn pots regularly, ideally at least once a week

In addition to the above, plants should be sprayed regularly against aphids, Red Spider etc. and with a fungicide such as Benomyl ('Benlate') before going into their winter dormancy period.

Appendix

Cushion plants for rock gardens, raised beds and troughs

Androsace spp.	*carnea, hedraeantha*
Arenaria spp.	*montana, nevadensis, tetraquetra*
Armeria spp.	*caespitosa, maritima*
Dianthus spp.	*erinaceus, freynii, haematocalyx, microlepis, pinifolius, petraeus*
Douglasia spp.	*laevigata, vitaliana*
Draba spp.	*aizoides, bryoides, dedeana, rigida, mollissima, polytricha* if covered with glass in winter.
Gypsophila	*aretioides* – may need winter cover
Saxifraga spp.	numerous, including most of the sub-section Porophyllum which includes European and Asian Kabschia types. Himalayan species will need cover in winter.
Scleranthus spp.	*biflorus, uniflorus*
Silene	*acaulis*

Cushion plants for cold frames or raised plunge beds
All the species listed above plus the following:

Androsace spp.	all the cushion forming species, of which there are more than twenty, can be successfully grown under this method.
Bolax	*gummifera*
Colobanthus spp.	*buchanani, canaliculatus*
Eritrichium spp.	*nanum* – a challenge!
Hectorella	*caespitosa*
Kelseya	*uniflora*
Primula spp.	*allionii, minima*
Pygmaea	*pulvinaris*
Sagina	*boydii*

Cushion plants for the alpine house
Species listed above plus the following:

Asyneuma	*pulvinaris*
Dionysia spp.	*aretioides, curviflora, janthina, tapetodes*
Haastia	*pulvinaris*
Raoulia spp.	*bryoides, eximia, mammillaris, rubra*

All of these species are difficult to grow and it would be advisable to grow some of the plants in the earlier lists before attempting them.

Bulbs for the Bleak Days

by Jack Elliott

The period from November until mid-March has little to commend it to gardeners, but there are a surprising number of bulbous plants which will flower during these bleak days, on the rock garden or in woodland conditions among shrubs. Three genera in particular can be relied upon to provide colour from Autumn until Spring: *Crocus, Cyclamen* and *Galanthus*.

In addition to these, colchicums will add to the display in the Autumn, but are usually past their best by November, and, after Christmas, irises, narcissus, and some of the smaller genera begin their season. All these bulbs make wonderful subjects for the cold greenhouse, but only those which will succeed in the open will be considered here.

In November the autumn flowering crocus species are at their best and may well continue until the New Year. Bulb catalogues offer a considerable number of them, all very desirable, including such well-known and easy species as *Crocus medius*, with deep lavender flowers and conspicuous orange stigmas, the darker *C. speciosus*, and the beautiful pale lilac, white-throated, *C. kotschyanus* var. *leucopharynx*. Other less common species which thrive in the open are *C. goulimyi*, pale lavender with an exceptionally long perianth tube; its exquisite white form *C. goulimyi* 'Alba', only recently becoming available; *C. banaticus*, which has unique iris-shaped lavender flowers; *C. laevigatus* with white to deep lavender flowers feathered outside with purple, and the large flowered white *C. boryi*.

The most widely grown autumn flowering cyclamen is *C. hederifolium* (syn. *neapolitanum*), which flourishes and seeds itself around even in dry shade, with pink or white flowers in September-October and delightfully patterned leaves from then until the following June. *Cyclamen cilicium* with smaller pale pink flowers, and its tiny white-flowered subspecies *intaminatum*, are also perfectly easy outside in partial shade.

Snowdrops may epitomise early spring flowers but their season begins in November or even earlier with *Galanthus nivalis* ssp. *reginae-olgae* (syn. *G. corcyrensis*), resembling the common Snow-drop (*G. nivalis*) except in flowering period. Following this there is often a gap in the season until February, when their full flush begins. For the galanthophile there are species and varieties galore, identifiable by differences in the leaves and subtly distinct flower markings. To the average gardener there are lots of beautiful Snowdrops, with a few obviously distinct species. The early-flowering *G. elwesii* is very large with handsome broad glaucous leaves. *G. ikariae* ssp. *latifolius* is very distinct in having broad glossy green leaves. *G. nivalis* 'Flavescens' is unusual in flower colour, the spots on the segments being yellow instead of green. This is uncommon but not difficult to grow.

Among the first bulbs to appear in January are the reticulate irises. *Iris histrioides* 'Major' is a wonderful plant with robust dark blue flowers and pale markings on the lip, withstanding bad weather, including snow and severe frosts, remarkably well. Recently there has been some variation in the cultivars of *I. histrioides* available, 'Lady Beatrix Stanley' being particularly good, but all are fine plants easily grown in gritty soil in a sunny spot. *Iris histrio* seems more difficult in the open but its variety *aintabensis* does equally well, with smaller pale blue flowers. A little later two yellow-flowered species appear. *Iris danfordiae* has squat flowers with reduced standards and tends to split up into tiny bulbs which fail to flower in later years. *Iris winogradowii* is a far superior species, like a yellow *I. histrioides* 'Major', but flowering later and preferring a moister partially shaded position. *Iris* 'Katherine Hodgkin' is a hybrid between *I. histrioides* and *I. winogradowii*, which flowers after the former is over. The plant is very vigorous, increasing rapidly in the garden, with large flowers of a strange mixture of pale blue, yellow and green which appeals to many growers.

Later still appear *I. reticulata* and its various cultivars, which can be found listed extensively in catalogues. The type plant has dark violet-blue flowers, 'Cantab' is pale blue, and 'Krelagii' purple. There are many others, originally derived from collected plants, which vary enormously in the wild, or from hybridisation with *I. histrioides*. All are outstandingly beautiful and all do well in freely-drained soil in a sunny position.

Most of the dwarf narcissi seem to flourish in partial shade with abundant humus, preferably leaf mould. Such conditions are ideal for *N. cyclamineus*, *N. triandrus*, *N. bulbocodium* and their hybrids. Just as there is one November-flowering Snowdrop, so there is one easily grown Narcissus which can be relied upon to flower well before Christmas, *N. minus* 'Cedric Morris', a typical miniature "Trumpet Daffodil", but a little taller than the otherwise similar *N. asturiensis* which usually starts flowering in February and is one of the best garden species. The "Hoop-petticoat" narcissi, *NN. bulbocodium*, *cantabricus* and *romieuxii* also flower very early. *N. cantabricus* varieties do best under glass, but *N. romieuxii*, although hailing from North Africa and flowering in January, will grow well in the garden, as will its very similar hybrid, 'Nylon'. Though not as pale as *N. cantabricus*, these have very pale yellow flowers with prominent anthers. The varieties of *N. bulbocodium* flower a little later and are excellent garden plants, even growing well in grass. Generally they have deep yellow flowers, but in the variety 'Citrinus' they are pale yellow.

Another exquisite group of narcissi are the "Angels Tears", *N. triandrus* and its forms and hybrids, with segments reflexing over the corona in a most attractive manner. The most commonly available form is *N. triandrus* 'Albus', with creamy-white flowers, but 'Concolor' is sometimes offered which has deep yellow flowers.

Narcissus cyclamineus has, as its name suggests, a long narrow corona with acutely reflexed segments. Its dainty little flowers can be seen in enormous abundance in the Meadow and Wild Garden at the Royal Horticultural Society's garden at Wisley. It probably needs moister conditions than most species to increase well.

Some good autumn-flowering crocus species have been mentioned, and in early Spring the choice is even wider. A visit to the Wisley Alpine House in February gives some idea of the great number available, especially the many different cultivars of *C. chrysanthus* and *C. vernus*. These grow perfectly well in the open garden as do many of the other species. *Crocus tommasinianus* is too well-known to need description, but it has one or two varieties which are less excessively prodigal with their seedlings. *C.* 'Whitewell Purple' is a good dark form, and *C. tommasinianus* 'Albus' is an uncommon but excellent white. Another white species, which is only now becoming common, is *C. malyii* with large white flowers and conspicuous red anthers. It does well in the open garden. *C. fleischeri* is delightful, with much smaller white flowers but even more prominent red anthers.

Among the yellow-flowered species, *C. flavus* is very reliable, with deep golden flowers unmarked on the outsides of the segments. *C. korolkowii* is similar but is flecked with dark brown on the exterior. This feathering is a conspicuous feature of some of the "blue" species, especially *CC. corsicus, minimus* and *imperati*. These all have flowers of pale to deep lavender, with conspicuous dark veining on the reverse of the segments. *C. imperati* flowers very early, and *C. corsicus* very late.

Cyclamen come into their own again in February when the varieties of *C. coum* start flowering. This name now covers a great range of plants, which have in the past been split according to the presence and absence of particular leaf markings and flower shape and colour, into different species. All are well worth growing and will flourish in partial shade with humus. Like *C. hederifolium*, they will seed themselves around when happy. Flower colour can be anything from white to deep magenta.

Having briefly considered the larger genera of bulbous plants, there are still several others with a few excellent winter flowering species; notably *Eranthis, Leucojum* and *Anemone*. Winter Aconites are invaluable for producing broad masses of colour under shrubs very early in the year. *Eranthis hyemalis* is the commonest species, rapidly naturalising to carpet the ground with deep yellow flowers in January. Another to look out for is *Eranthis* 'Guinea Gold', a splendid hybrid with much larger flowers, which unfortunately seems to have become uncommon.

Leucojum vernum, the Spring Snowflake, flowers soon after the Winter Aconites are over. Surprisingly it seems less popular than the Snowdrops, although enjoying the same conditions of moist shade, even in grass. It has glossy green leaves and 15–20cm stems bearing one or two large cup-shaped hanging white flowers with conspicuous green spots at the tips, or yellow in the variety *carpathicum*.

Many of the Anemones are a little later flowering but *A. blanda* and its cultivars usually begin to unfurl their flowers in February. Although often said to require a sunny position they seem to be perfectly happy in partial shade. The relatively large flowers are held only a few centimetres above the deeply cut leaves, and can be blue, white, or pink. They are among the best of early bulbs.

Sterling Silvers

by Chris Norton

'Sterling Silvers' suggests a sense of solid worth in a group of plants grown chiefly for their foliage effect. It is also a reference to the 'new half crown' reputedly fished out at the show bench by judges of yore as the perfect standard for colour. Both these concepts are valid; certainly no rock garden would be complete without its share of silver plants, whilst the best of the pot grown show 'silvers' can match the coin for brilliance.

Silver colour is usually due to a covering of fine hairs; in some plants short and close giving a velvety appearance, in others long and silky. The perception of silver colour is subjective, some varieties are more or less grey, in others the overlay of white hairs does not wholly conceal the basic green of the leaves.

The seemingly excessive development of plant hairs is an adaptation to reduce water loss and a protection against the increased level of ultra-violet radiation from sunlight at high altitude. Plant species which have made such adaptations might be expected to produce difficulties in cultivation, and in general silver plants do require special care. For the most part they are sun lovers which thrive in gritty, well drained soils with a relatively low nutrient level.

In the garden, scree conditions or raised beds are ideal for many species, with abundant water in the growing season. Many 'silvers' dislike wet winter conditions, and overhead protection with a pane of glass is worth considering for some of these. For the most difficult species, winter survival is more assured with pot culture in frames or a well ventilated greenhouse. Large gardens sometimes feature silver beds or borders, but for the rock garden, individual specimens are generally interspersed amongst the other plants. Here they provide endless possibilities for colour combinations and contrasts. As with all rock plants which can disappear after a hard winter, propagation of 'silvers' should be a routine annual procedure to provide replacement stock, plus a few spares for exchange with other enthusiasts.

Space limits the number of varieties which can be considered in this article and the following is a personal selection, concentrating on those which are most readily available.

Starting with two easily grown shrubs: *Convolvulus cneorum* will thrive in a well drained garden border, but, hailing from southern Europe, it is questionably hardy and benefits from the shelter of a wall or, better still, a dark evergreen hedge. Rarely more than 60cm high, the stems bearing whorls of lanceolate leaves are crowned in July with a succession of large white trumpets striped on the outside with pale pink. Judicious pruning helps to keep the plant compact, and cuttings taken in August root readily to provide hostages against particularly severe winters. A superb introduction from high in South Africa's Drakensberg Mountains, *Euryops acraeus* combines bright silver-blue foliage with clear yellow daisies. The plant is fully hardy and forms a 45cm high dome, 60cm or more in width. This is one of the few 'silvers' which will thrive in damper situations, and a light airy situation in the peat bed will probably produce a better specimen than the usual sharply drained rock garden.

Another silver to light up the peat bed is *Leucogenes leontopodium*, the New Zealand Edelweiss. This plant prefers half shade, at least in the southern half of Britain where fine specimens are hard to find. Humid conditions further north encourage more vigorous growth and the production of the quite large yellow 'flannel flowers'.

Where space permits, *Salix lanata* is a very desirable shrub with its woolly silver buds and leaves and 5cm yellow catkins set off to perfection by the dark stems. The variety *stuartii* is perhaps the best form, for it seldom exceeds 60cm and has larger catkins and smaller leaves than the type. This plant also prefers high humidity and a moist root run which can be provided by an adjacent large rock.

Two silver plants which no garden should be without are *Leucanthemum hosmariense*, with its deeply cut leaves and large white yellow-eyed daisies generously provided in a long succession throughout summer and autumn, and *Tanacetum densum* 'amani' (*Chrysanthemum haradjanii*). The leaves of the latter are closely pectinate with each segment narrowly crenulate. This gives a feathery appearance usually likened to silver filigree. The bright dome or mat of foliage is not enhanced by the scattering of rather dowdy yellow flowers which can well be removed. A related species, *Tanacetum herderi* makes a neat bush. All three are sun lovers which revel in an open spot in well drained soil.

The genus *Artemisia*, the Wormwoods of Europe or Sagebrush of America, has a number of desirable species which prefer the same conditions. *A.A. canescens, glacialis, pedemontana* and *schmidtiana* 'Nana' all have much-dissected foliage, whilst *A. stellerana*, variously known as 'Mori's Form' or 'Boughton Silver', has almost white leaves like a Chrysanthemum. This is a vigorous mat-forming plant which will quickly swamp its smaller neighbours and could well be confined to a crack in paving or a place beside a path. There are a number of other mat-forming 'silvers', two of which are amongst the New Zealand Scabweeds. *Raoulia australis* has tiny leaves no more than 2mm long, whilst *R. hookeri* has larger leaves in rosettes. Both species have rooting stems which form a prostrate mat and both share a dislike for winter wet. A coarse carpeter which needs careful siting so as not to overgrow choicer plants is *Lamium maculatum* 'Beacon Silver'. This Dead-nettle has bright silver leaves edged with green and heads of mauve flowers.

Rather more select is *Achillea ageratifolia*, a Yarrow from Greece, which displays large white flower heads on 15cm stems above narrow, crimped and deeply cut silver leaves. *Antennaria dioica* 'Minima' is another useful mat-forming plant with many upright stems bearing heads of pink flowers over woolly leaves.

The genus *Helichrysum* provides more outstanding silver plants than any other. *H. milfordiae* forms a shallow cushion or mat with dense rosettes of furry, silvery leaves. In spring, large crimson buds develop into white stemless 'everlasting' flowers. Old flower heads are best removed carefully and the plant should be covered with a pane of glass against the winter rains. *H. sibthorpii* (syn. *virgineum*) is best known for the springtime combination of salmon-pink buds set against broad grey felted leaves. The flowers which follow are, by comparison, a disappointing pale yellow. Usually grown under glass, the plant is hardy and well worth trying outside. *H. splendidum* (syn. *trilineatum, alveolatum*) rivals the best silver plants for colour, but at 100cm grows too tall for many rock gardens. The same may be said of *H. italicum* (syn. *angusti-folium*) with its delicious scent of curry. Fortunately both plants can safely be cut back to within 15cm of the ground in early spring, and the resulting young growth is tidier and of better colour.

Amongst the aristocrats of the alpine plant world there is a wide choice of fine silver foliage plants. These are treasures for the alpine house or, at some risk, for a trough or raised bed which can be covered in winter. They are not so easily acquired as the foregoing selection; watch the seed lists, visit specialist nurseries and plant stalls at the AGS shows, and contact other enthusiasts for possible exchanges. Here are six of the best to conclude: –

Veronica bombycina from high screes in the Lebanon has such a dense covering of hairs that both the short stems and small obovate leaves appear white. Flattish, china-blue flowers in May are too pale to provide much of a contrast. The plant should be trimmed occasionally to keep it compact. All watering is best carried out from below, and very little is required through the winter.

The Cretan Dittany or Marjoram, *Origanum dictamnus* forms a 20cm dome of wiry stems bearing opposite, rounded leaves densely felted above and below. Rose coloured flowers like tiny hops are long lasting in summer.

Convolvulus boissieri (syn. *nitidus*) from limestone rocks in southern Spain is a mat-forming plant with a shiny, metallic quality to the silver of its leaves. These are narrow, oval in shape, folded along the midrib and deeply veined so that the light glistens on the closely pressed covering of silky hairs. In cultivation, the plant is not very free with its typical white Bindweed flowers.

How does a humble Plantain come to be included in such distinguished company? Certainly *Plantago nivalis* is the least refined of these last six plants, but it is an easy and attractive beginner's silver for the alpine house. Outside, the long silky hairs become soggy with winter rain and the plants rarely survive. They are readily grown from seed in a gritty compost, and require potting on fairly frequently. In early spring, the very dark buds gradually lengthening into typical plantain 'flowers' make a strong contrast with the neat rosette of pale leaves.

A cushion plant from New Zealand which is becoming increasingly popular is *Raoulia* x *logani*, a naturally occurring hybrid thought to be a cross between *Raoulia rubra* and *Leucogenes leontopodium*. The tight woolly rosettes give this the look of a crevice or scree plant, and whilst perfect drainage is essential, much water is required in the growing season.

Lastly, an old favourite, *Androsace vandellii*. Two earlier names for this plant indicate its character, *A. imbricata* for the imbricate or overlapping appearance of the leaves arranged in rosettes, and *A. argentea* for the silver colour imparted by the dense covering of minute, star-shaped hairs. This is a crevice dweller with a scattered distribution in volcanic rocks of the Alps and Pyrenees. Small cushions are relatively easily grown from seed using a very gritty compost. Prick out a large batch of seedlings and select those with the tightest rosette formation and best flowers, for the plant is variable. Growing the seedlings on to specimen size presents a challenge, but the results justify all the attention necessary, for the silver dome is a pleasure during the whole year, only surpassed when the foliage is entirely hidden by a sheet of white flowers in spring.

Shrubs for All Seasons

by Barry N. Starling

In the mountains shrubs, which are plants with woody stems, are as much a part of the scene as the cushion plants which we recognise as being typically alpine. Indeed, some shrubs will assume the cushion shape, being low mounds of intricately branched twigs extending their perimeters by, perhaps, less than a centimetre a year. As the altitude increases so the shrubs adapt to cope with the more rigorous conditions, so that a willow, for instance, will become dwarfed and may cover its leaves with silky, silvery hairs to reduce moisture loss to the ever present wind. Even higher, the branches may creep along the ground and over rocks to take advantage of the shelter such positions afford.

It is the great diversity of these adaptations that makes alpine shrublets interesting and attractive enough for us to want to include them in our alpine gardens. For these are the 'furniture' of a rock garden which, though forming permanent structures, are continually changing in appearance with the seasons.

Shrubs can be evergreen, retaining their leaves throughout the year, or deciduous, in which case the leaves fall in autumn to be replaced by new leaves in spring. Please do not be tempted to discount the latter group for their winter nudity. So often newcomers to shrub gardening confine their choice to evergreens, complaining that, "there are nothing but bare sticks in winter on deciduous bushes". We have already mentioned the willows, which are of course deciduous – consider the quaintly gnarled branchlets of *Salix* x *boydii*, or curvy stems of the prostrate *S. arbuscula*. Such features can be enjoyed in winter when there are no patches of strident colour to distract one's gaze. The tracery of fine branches of the dwarf Japanese maples, *Acer palmatum* 'Dissectum' and its forms, mushrooming from stout little trunks, is frequently enhanced by glistening white frost. Similarly, it is primarily when frost outlines the fishbone filigree of the branchlets of *Ulmus parvifolia* 'Pygmaea', the Dwarf Elm, that its intricate formation attracts our attention. Yet these features are a bonus because the willows have their catkins, the maples their delicately cut foliage and the Elm a pattern of tiny, fresh green leaves in spring, and all produce a grand finale in autumn of butter yellow, flaming crimson or rich gold fall colour.

Among the deciduous rhododendrons, *R. canadense (Rhodora canadensis)* is no sensation in flower, producing myriads of tiny pink blossoms on a twiggy shrub barely 50cm high. In autumn, however, the older leaves turn to thunder-cloud purple, forming a sensational backing to the sunset colours of younger leaves. Of the dwarf barberries, *Berberis thunbergii* 'Atropurpurea Nana' (*B.* 'Little Favourite'), sports red-budded, yellow flowers among the unfolding red leaves. The maroon-red of the leaves is maintained throughout the summer until they flare into brilliant scarlet before falling. On mature plants sealing-wax-red berries are left to decorate the spiny skeleton into winter. As a garden plant how much more worthwhile is this than, for instance, the small evergreen *Hebe* 'Carl Teschner' which dons a beautiful blue gown for two weeks of the summer, but remains for the rest of the year in a drab green uniform.

Of course, in a large garden, space can be afforded for a shrub which only gives of its best for two weeks of the year – indeed, a planting of *Hebe* 'Carl Teschner' together with *Berberis thunbergii* 'Atropurpurea Nana' and, for example, one of the golden foliage heathers such as *Calluna vulgaris* 'Gold Carpet' will give constantly changing combinations of colour with several highlights during the year.

For mid-winter flower colour, only *Erica herbacea (carnea)* among the smaller shrubs is brave enough to bloom through snow and ice regardless. There are now many cultivars of this species and on all but the largest rock gardens great care must be taken to avoid the more rampant ones. Possibly the smallest is one with rich, wine-red flowers, *E. h.* 'Eileen Porter', but my favourite, which is slightly larger growing, is the old cultivar *E. h.* 'Vivellii', which combines deep red flowers with bronzy-red tips to the foliage, so that even out of flower it is worth a second glance.

Small enough for the smallest rock garden or, even better, peat garden, are two shrubs related to *Erica*. One is the tiny, mat-forming *Arcterica nana* which, in the form 'Redshank', pushes up from among minute, dark green leaves, short red stems bearing red buds which open in late winter as creamy-white miniature globes clasped by red calyces. The other is a dwarf version of the Cranberry, *Oxycoccus macrocarpon* 'Hamilton'. As the cold weather approaches its evergreen leaves assume a warm browny-red hue, greening again when spring comes. In summer, short wiry stems dangle pinky-white pixie hats which, in theory, should give way to large scarlet cranberries, but my plant has yet to yield this bonus.

That a shrub flowers against the rigours of winter is undoubtedly credit-worthy. When that shrub is also possessed of a delightful fragrance it is surely worthy of a place on the rock garden even if its habit of growth is a little eccentric. *Daphne blagayana* is a wanderer. It is happiest when left to scramble through and beneath its neigbours so that its bare, unattractive stems are mainly hidden from view while its clusters of white flowers, framed by a collar of dark green leaves, poke forth here and there to be enjoyed for several weeks during late winter.

Towards the end of winter other species of *Daphne* will flower, together with a handful of the smaller *Rhododendron* species. The glory of such early flowering rhododendrons as *RR. mucronulatum, dauricum, moupinense*, 'Seta', etc., can be short-lived if night frosts are more than a degree or two. Grown in pots and brought into the alpine house to flower they can be enjoyed for much longer.

The months of April, May and June bring forth a bonanza of colour. Rhododendrons are joined by their relatives in the family Ericaceae such as *Andromeda, Cassiope, Phyllodoce, Kalmia, Ledum, Leiophyllum, Kalmiopsis, Menziesia* and many more. Gold is contributed by the smaller berberis, genistas and cytisus – silver from the foliage of such treasures as *Helichrysum coralloides*, with coral-like stems or *Euryops acraeus* from the Drakensberg Mountains of S. Africa. Solid blocks of colour are provided by shocking pink, ruby-red or sky-blue penstemons, while the small and dainty prunus species such as the Dwarf Almond, *Prunus tenella*, the double white *P. glandulosa* 'Albiplena' or pink *P. prostrata* (which only remains prostrate so long as it is nibbled by a goat!) add pink or white airiness to the scene.

For those clever enough to grow them, *Ceanothus prostratus* and *C. pumilus* will add blue to the palette in the form of fluffy blue heads over a matt-green carpet or low evergreen mound. Much easier is *C. thyrsiflorus* 'Repens', but with an eventual spread of

16. *Saxifraga oppositifolia*

17. *Kalmiopsis leachiana*

18. *Armeria caespitosa*

perhaps 2 metres and height of nearly a metre this shrub will be too large for most rock gardens. The shrubby or sub-shrubby lithodoras (lithospermums) yield, in *L. diffusa* 'Heavenly Blue' or 'Grace Ward', a most intense blue on prostrate mats, or charming pastel-blue on the silky-leaved shrublets of *L. oleifolia*, while the Hedgehog Broom, *Erinacea anthyllis (pungens)* clouds the tips of spiny branches with misty-blue pea flowers.

So great and so tempting is the range of spring-flowering shrubs that often, as flaming June fades the last of their flowers, the rock garden becomes drab, leaving a feeling of anti-climax to the beholder. It is at this time that a range of very easy, sun-loving small shrubs come onto the scene with their brilliant colours. The helianthemums now offer a bewildering selection of crimson, yellow, tawny-gold, brick-orange, rose-pink, pale pink or white, single or double flowers needing no more than a trim over after flowering to keep the bushes compact. Closely related *Halimium ocymoides* is a little larger and more upright, sporting golden "Dogroses" each with a chestnut-brown eye.

For length of flowering period few small shrubs can rival *Potentilla arbuscula*. This is a high alpine counterpart of *P. fruticosa*, a shrub widespread throughout the Northern Hemisphere. *P. arbuscula* forms at 5000m in the Himalayas, low pancakes of silver-sheened, hairy foliage sprinkled through summer with flat, round, golden flowers. In the garden its stature is a little higher and flowering lasts from May to October. Also yellow and summer flowering are the hypericums, some of the choicest of which are unfortunately a little tender. *H. olympicum (polyphyllum)*, however, is a tough little shrub bearing gold or sulphur-coloured blooms above neat grey-green leaves. Fiery-hot *Rhododendron nakaharae* often blooms into July while the snow-white bells of *Zenobia pulverulenta* are produced gracefully on a taller shrub, both enjoying a moist, peaty soil. In such a soil the low, suckering shoots of *Philesia magellanica (buxifolia)* can sometimes be persuaded to produce exotic, 5cm long, tubular crimson bells from summer into autumn. Unusual in its flower colour is the Californian *Mimulus glutinosus* which performs throughout the summer months with Musk flowers of warm terracotta. Contrast this with the cool-white, tubular bells dangled from tips of arching stems of *Leucothoe keiskei*.

Summer continues with a fascinating range of hebes or parahebes in diverse forms of habit, leaf-shape and colour, mostly with blue, lavender or white flower spikes. Spiraeas with heads of pink or crimson can be found in the small forms of *S. japonica* such as 'Bullata', 'Alpina' or 'Little Princess'. A choice relative of the spiraeas is *Petrophytum hendersonii*, which very slowly makes a silver-grey dome of 15cm diameter suitable for the smallest rock garden or trough. In its lofty alpine habitat it enjoys cool, moist air and will thrive best in the garden in a position out of the baking sun. Its flowers are small, fluffy, white moppets borne just above the cushion. *Ptilotrichum spinosum* makes a large silver dome of up to 45cm diameter with white or pink flowers like those of Sweet Alyssum, its close relative. Towards late summer the gently spreading *Ceratostigma plumbaginoides* thrusts up large cluster heads of bright blue, ever increasing in contrast to the foliage as autumn turns the leaves to deep crimson.

Autumn is the time for berries and it is then that the closely related gaultherias, pernettyas and vacciniums come into their own with a colour range that includes white, pink, red, blue, lavender and purple. A number of these are very worthy flowering plants and the vacciniums in particular add red or chocolate coloured new growth to their list of attributes. These all thrive best in an acid soil but the creeping cotoneasters, low, thicket-forming *Sorbus reducta* and smaller berberis species which produce scarlet, pink or orange fruits are less demanding of special soil conditions.

In addition to the shrubs described here there are many more of equal merit, not to mention the dwarf conifers which are described in the next chapter. Together they provide all-year-round interest as well as giving that air of permanence which is such an essential feature of all successful rock gardens.

Why Grow Dwarf Conifers?

by A. R. Woodliffe

In painting landscapes the artist uses certain subjects for focal points. When creating a new rock garden the same need arises and dwarf conifers can supply the focal points, often adding height to a flat site or cushioning the top of a rock outcrop.

The choosing of varieties is very important, only the miniature ones being suitable for the smaller sized gardens which most of us have today. They should be true dwarfs which reach only 30cm or so in height at maturity, there being no place in the rock garden for plants artificially dwarfed as in the art of Bonsai.

The use of dwarf conifers in rockeries and alpine gardens suggests an alpine atmosphere, their evergreen forms setting off the low growing flora around them. Anyone who has attempted alpine gardening without them will be surprised at the improvement brought about by the introduction of a few well chosen varieties.

The choice is much wider than it was a decade ago, many new dwarf forms of a range of genera, but particularly pines and hemlocks (*Tsuga sp.*), having been introduced. Some of the most miniature forms are to be found in the *Chamaecyparis* group, especially among the varieties of Japanese Hinoki Cypress (*Chamaecyparis obtusa*). These form delightful little buns that may take 30 years to reach 30cm diameter. There are also very attractive miniature forms of spruces, particularly the Canadian White Spruce (*Picea glauca*), while the Canadian Hemlock (*Tsuga canadensis*) has similarly provided some really compact varieties suitable for troughs.

The pines, although mostly towering forest trees in their normal forms, provide us with dwarfs giving great architectural value.

The cultural needs of dwarf conifers are not complex. Given a well drained and not too rich soil they will, like most alpines, retain their dwarf stature. In hot weather spraying with water is helpful and, as with all evergreens, careful attention should be paid to watering throughout the season following planting. The only serious pests are Red Spider mites on the spruces (*Picea spp.*) and Woolly Aphis on the pines. Both can be controlled with a systemic spray in summer.

A list of reliable, truly dwarf varieties follows, those which are especially suitable for troughs being marked with an asterisk (*).

Chamaecyparis lawsoniana 'Green Globe'
Forms a tight bun of rich, dark green foliage.

Chamaecyparis lawsoniana 'Minima Aurea'
An attractive conical golden form keeping its colour throughout the year.

**Chamaecyparis obtusa* 'Intermedia'
A dense emerald green globe with cupped foliage.

**Chamaecyparis obtusa* 'Juniperoides Compacta'
A flattened bun of yellow-green foliage. Very slow growing.

Chamaecyparis obtusa 'Nana'
An old cultivar of very slow growth, producing a dense, flat-topped dark green bush.

Chamaecyparis pisifera 'Tsukumi'
A tiny mid-green bun from Japan.

Chamaecyparis thyoides 'Heatherbun'
A slow growing form that changes to a rich plum purple in winter.

Cryptomeria japonica 'Compressa'
Makes a globe shaped tight packed plant, the tips of the shoots turning rich red bronze in winter.

Juniperus communis 'Compressa'
The Noah's Ark Juniper; a perfect column of blue-green.

Picea abies 'Gregoryana'
A form akin to a hedgehog – a prickly mound of grey-green needles.

**Picea abies* 'Little Gem'
A light green, dense mass of fine small needles.

The following three forms of Canadian White Spruce are all

derived from *Picea glauca* 'Albertiana Conica', itself a dwarf, but are all much smaller. They arose as bud sports which, when propagated, maintained their dwarf characteristics.

Picea glauca 'Alberta Globe'
A flat growing cushion of mid green colour.

Picea glauca 'Laurin'
A true miniature cone shape.

Picea glauca 'Tiny'
As its name suggests, a very tight bun form.

Pinus leucodermis 'Schmidtii'
A remarkable, slow growing pine only 45cm high after 40 years growth.

Pinus mugo 'Humpy'
A squat, very attractive little plant with dark green needles and red winter buds.

Pinus mugo 'Kissen'
A dense, flat-topped bun with short, dark green needles.

Pinus sylvestris 'Frensham'
A blue-green mound attractive at all times.

Pinus sylvestris 'Gold Medal'
A conical dwarf turning a rich gold in the winter months.

Thuja occidentalis 'Caespitosa'
A small, low-growing plant with irregular, congested foliage.

Thuja orientalis 'Aurea Nana'
This golden *Thuja* should be in every garden – a very popular, good form.

Tsuga canadensis 'Minuta'
A minute form with small, mid-green leaves and a congested, irregular branching habit.

Tsuga canadensis 'Nearing'
Upright twiggy growth with congested shoots.

Tsuga canadensis 'Palomino'
A flat, compact globe with small light green leaves.

Plants for Shady Corners

by Richard Bird

Growing plants in the shade has always been considered one of the greatest problems confronting gardeners. It *is* a problem but only in as much as it is difficult to decide how to limit one's choice of plants from the multitude that grow in such a situation.

Before considering the plants themselves, it is necessary to look at the types of shade and shade conditions in which they grow in the wild and relate these to situations found in the garden. Shade can vary depending on the amount of light and sunlight reaching it. Semi-shaded conditions are provided when light and sunbeams are slightly filtered throughout the day by branches and thin foliage giving the soil and plants a dappled appearance. Partial shade is provided in east- or west-facing situations where the sun only shines for part of the day. Again, shade is found in north-facing situations which receive no direct sun but which, not being directly overhung, receive ambient daylight. Finally, areas in full shade are those which receive no sunlight and very little daylight; this is the most difficult situation in which to grow plants.

There are other conditions that are important besides the level of light. Moisture must have careful consideration, as at the base of walls and under trees the soil can be too dry to support plants. Many of the woodland plants to be described later require a peaty soil so the presence of limey soil will affect what you can grow.

Moving back to the wild, we can now relate the above conditions to plants in their native habitats. Starting at the lower levels there are the woodland plants which grow in the rich leafmould. These plants grow mainly on the fringes of woods or where the trees are thin enough to allow in dappled light. The plants usually grow in a thick layer of leafmould, which not only supplies them with adequate moisture but also an abundant supply of nutrients, an important factor to be remembered. Back in the deeper shade are plants which have adapted themselves to complete their annual cycle before the trees have put on their green mantle. This means that they must make the most of the early spring when they can get plenty of light and water which the summer canopy will deny them. A common example of this is our native Bluebell. Most woodland plants are, strictly speaking, too large to be considered rock plants, but most alpine gardeners grow at least some and many have complete beds devoted to them.

If we move up the mountain we come to the scrubby areas where the trees have disappeared but we still have bushes providing light shade. Further up on the mountainside one could be forgiven for believing that there would be no shade but a moment's reflection will show this is not so. On a large scale there is the north side of the mountain which will either receive no sun or just a little during certain times of the day. On a much smaller scale, even a tiny rock will cast a shadow on its north side, of which some plants may have taken advantage. On these rocky heights the plants are usually true alpines but it is still possible to find woodland plants tucked under rocks. A close examination of the limestone pavements of our own country will soon show how woodland plants can adapt themselves to growing in the fissures between the rocks. The conditions are not that far removed from their normal habitat in that the crevices not only provide shade but also moisture and nutrients in the humus and detritus that is naturally collected in the cracks of the rocks. Many other shade plants can be found growing on the banks of streams or in shady ravines.

In the garden we can provide conditions that would suit most of the plants that grow in the above situations. Shady peat beds can be constructed to care for the woodlanders, small trees and shrubs, and carefully positioned rocks can provide for those plants of a more open position. So let us now look at the various opportunities that the garden provides for growing shade plants. Rock gardens and raised beds are usually constructed in full sun, but there will always be odd pockets of shade that will be eminently suitable for growing plants that prefer these conditions. Very few shade loving plants like a really dry situation, so while the compost should be gritty and well drained, it should also contain an extra quantity of leafmould or peat to ensure that it is a bit more moisture retentive than the surrounding bed. Shrubs should be carefully sited so that they not only provide an architectural structure to the bed, but also a variety of shade conditions to allow the maximum amount of different situations in which to grow plants. Many beds will be in partial shade for some of the day, shaded by fences, walls or distant trees but if this is not too excessive then a wide range of plants can be grown as many of the sun-loving species will tolerate a modicum of shade and only those that require hot scree conditions need be excluded. However it should be remembered that sun-lovers rarely flower so freely in shade and can be more prone to diseases such as rusts and mildews.

If the shade is more dense then further thought must be given. The most likely candidates to grow here are woodlanders which are used to such conditions in the wild, indeed they are not only used to such conditions but actually need them as the naked sun would be too much for them. They are used to having their roots in rich moist humus so the ground must be carefully prepared with the addition of extra peat and leafmould. Trees providing dense shade can be a great problem. Deep rooted trees with a relatively open canopy such as Oak can be underplanted with care but shallow rooted, close canopied trees such as Beech prove most difficult. Not only do the leaves prevent the sunlight reaching the ground but they also prevent the rain penetrating and the shallow roots quickly starve the soil of nutrients; very little will grow under these conditions.

The preparation of beds has been dealt with elsewhere in this volume so I will not repeat it except to say that when plants are obtained, find out as much as you can about the conditions in which they grow in the wild and then try and give them equivalent situations in your garden.

Now to the plants themselves. There are so many that the selection can only be partial and, to a certain extent, it must be a choice of personal favourites. Most are reasonably easy to grow and will not only give you good experience in growing shade-loving plants but hours of pleasure enjoying their beauty.

Woodlanders can provide us with a great range of garden plants. The United States of America and Japan provide us with two important spring flowering genera: *Trillium* and *Erythronium*. Probably the best known of the trilliums is *T. grandiflorum*, commonly known as Wake Robin. Like all trilliums, its parts come in threes; three petals, three sepals and three leaves. The most frequently seen form has pure white flowers, but it is variable, one of the best forms being the pink one that can be seen at Edinburgh Botanic Garden. There are also double forms. While a single clump can look very attractive, the ultimate is to have sheets of them, as they often grow in the wild, but this needs rather a large garden! *T. sessile* is quite widely available from nurseries but not very often seen in gardens. Again, when well grown, this can look spectacular, but whereas *T. grandiflorum*'s white flowers stand out in a dark corner, the dark red, erect petals and mottled leaves of *T. sessile* often need a shaft of light to bring out their beauty. The colour of the flower can be very variable, some not worth growing, so it is best to check that you are buying a good clone. The leaves are also variable, this time in the colour of their blotches, which can be either pale or dark. The plant rejoices under the name of Toad Trillium or Toad Shade. Another beautiful member of this genus with red petals is *T. erectum*, but they are quite different in appearance. Here the petals nestle between the sepals rather than standing proudly erect as in *T. sessile* and they lack the shiny lustre. There are many more trilliums such as the yellow *T. luteum* with its lovely scent or the dwarf species *Trillium nivale*, but if we stopped to look at all the interesting members of one genus we should be neglecting so many others.

Another mainly American genus that likes cool peaty soil in light shade is *Erythronium*. These are hardy bulbous plants with hanging, nodding flower heads with reflexed petals. They are usually either yellow, pink or a combination of both. One of the most commonly available is the European *E. dens-canis*, the Dog's Tooth Violet, which typically has pink flowers and beautiful mottled leaves. Another good pink species with mottled leaves is *E. revolutum*. *E. oregonum* has white or cream flowers with a deep yellow centre separated from the main colour of the petals by short red lines. The superb *E.* 'White Beauty' is thought to be a natural hybrid of this species and *E. citrinum* but it may be no more than a fine selected form of *E. oregonum*. It is well worth growing, having the ability to establish itself well and grow freely into large clumps, even on soils which are drier than those favoured by the more choosy species. There are quite a number of yellows and the hybrid 'Pagoda' is one of the best. This also grows freely and strongly, like one of its parents, *E. tuolumnense*, which is worth considering in its own right. There are many more to consider, the leaves of some giving as much pleasure as the flowers. As with most bulbs, the leaves do not last long after flowering.

It might be worth sticking with bulbs for a while. Snowdrops,

Galanthus spp., are something with which we are all familiar, too familiar perhaps as they often do not get a second glance. In spite of outward similarities there are quite a number of different species and seemingly hundreds of hybrids and cultivars. Another fact that sometimes comes as a surprise is the length of flowering season, the first, *G. nivalis* ssp. *reginae-olgae*, coming into flower in October. There are far too many different snowdrops to enumerate and describe here, but you will find great variety in size, markings, and time of flowering. They all have basically the same flower shape but some are double and some rarer ones (*G. nivalis* 'Lutescens', 'Flavescens' and 'Lady Elphinstone') have yellow markings in place of the normal green. Snowdrop bulbs should not be allowed to dry out completely and should be moved or bought while they are still in growth. Many good bulb nurseries offer a wide range 'in the green' in spring. Desiccated bulbs from a garden centre are much less likely to succeed.

A bulb that is often confused with the Snowdrop is the Snowflake, *Leucojum* spp. A close look will soon reveal, however, that there is only a superficial resemblance. The most immediate difference is that the Snowflake has six petals of equal length, the tips of which are green or sometimes yellow. *L. vernum* is about 15–20cm high and flowers in February and March; *L. aestivum* is much taller and flowers later. If they get the moist conditions that they both like they will soon multiply.

Another 'bulb' (tuber really) that should not be purchased dry is the Winter Aconite that brightens up many a dark corner in Spring. *Eranthis hyemalis* is the commonest with the form 'Guinea Gold' being the best if you can locate it.

Most of these plants are spring flowering as they will then get the sunlight before the woodland canopy develops. Three more examples of these include plants which are familiar in our own native woodlands: bluebells, anemones and primulas. I only include bluebells here by way of warning. Attractive as they may be in the vast sheets of blue that we often see in the wild, they can be a bit of a nuisance in the garden. Fine if you have a wood you can devote to them, but in a bed or border they seed and multiply at an alarming rate; often burying themselves deeply amongst other treasures making it impossible to extract them. Think carefully before you introduce them.

Wood anemones (*Anemone nemorosa*) can also spread at a surprising rate, given the right conditions, but they are much easier to control and they charm me so with their elegant simplicity that I don't think I would ever consider them a nuisance. There are quite a number of cultivars available including some blue forms ('Allenii', 'Robinsoniana') and a delightful double white, 'Vestal'. There are numerous other species besides our own native anemone, many preferring the sun, but there are still a lot that either prefer shade or will at least grow in it. One of the finer ones is *A. ranunculoides*. It quite closely resembles *A. nemorosa* except that, as its name implies, it is buttercup yellow. This also has a lovely double form. *AA. apennina* and *blanda* are similar in character. The type forms are blue but there are various shades of this as well as white and pink. Personally I prefer to have plants of only one colour together; a mixture looks too 'busy' and somehow 'unwoodlandlike'.

Hepatica is a genus closely related to *Anemone*; it was actually named *Anemone hepatica* until recently. The two commonest species are *H. nobilis* (syn. *triloba*) and *H. transsilvanica* (syn. *angulosa*). They resemble each other quite closely except that the latter is much larger in all its parts. The type forms are blue, but white, mauve and pink forms are found as well as some double ones which are not quite so easy to come by. These are delightful, starry little plants that are most welcome in the spring. They should be planted under deciduous bushes or trees where they receive spring sunshine, but avoid the fierce heat of summer.

In passing just now I mentioned primulas and, with some reluctance, I feel I must dwell a little longer on these delightful plants; reluctance because I am not certain where to begin, or indeed where to end. The Society has already published two full-scale monographs on the genus; one on the Asiatic and the other on the European and American species. These are essential for anyone who begins to get interested in the subject and I am sure that everyone does at sometime or another. Many of the Himalayan species prefer moist positions. Some of the candelabra types with tiers of flowers opening in succession are easy to grow including *P. japonica*, which happily sows itself and includes two good forms, 'Miller's Crimson' and 'Postford White'. *P. denticulata*, the so-called 'Drumstick Primula' is even easier and, like *P. japonica*, will self sow, but in order to keep good forms of these and other species it is essential to propagate vegetatively. *P. florindae*, the commonly named Himalayan Cowslip has beautiful sweetly scented yellow or orange flowers held in clusters atop metre-high stems. It comes readily from seed. *P. vialii* is rather spectacular, often being mistaken for an orchid. The flowers, borne in narrow spires on the 30cm stems, are lavender when open, scarlet in the unopened state at the tip of the spike. This is a short-lived species but comes freely from seed.

The European species will mostly tolerate drier conditions but still prefer light shade, a raised bed shaded by a tree for example. Our own *PP. vulgaris* and *veris* (Primrose and Cowslip) should not be despised and are not at all difficult to grow. Many of the *P. juliae* hybrids, which resemble primroses in appearance but are smaller in all their parts, are very attractive, although some such as 'Wanda' might be considered too common. The various cultivated forms of *P. auricula* are also common but include some marvellous plants, many of which have leaves covered with dust-like farina. Another species with this characteristic is *P. marginata* of which there are many varieties. In some the farina is concentrated along the edges of the leaf giving it the appearance of being edged with gold dust. There are another 500 or so species and probably several thousand varieties of primulas which could be discussed but obviously this is impossible. I have mentioned a few of the easiest to grow but when confidence has increased there is plenty of scope for delving into this fascinating genus.

One of the most spectacular plants in the spring is the double form of the Bloodroot, *Sanguinaria canadensis*. The bud emerges through the leafmould sheathed in a scalloped grey-green leaf. When the flower opens it is a ball of pure white petals; not long lasting but a glory while it does so. The single type form is not so breathtaking but has a charming elegance which makes it almost an equal to the double. The name 'Bloodroot' can readily be understood if you bruise or cut one of the thick rhizomatous 'roots', which will bleed a red sap. Not a very common plant, but it grows well in conditions that suit it, a moist peaty soil in semi or partial shade.

Gentians comprise a very large genus of about 400 species so it is not surprising that there are a few of these sun-lovers that will tolerate some shade. *G. asclepiadea*, the Willow Gentian, with tall arching stems, is the best known. This can be too tall for the rock garden; *G. septemfida* is shorter and will tolerate light shade as will the prostrate *G. sino-ornata* and its many hybrids. *G. sino-ornata* is easy to grow in rich lime-free soil and is also easy to propagate by simple division. It can provide an incredible splash of blue in the autumn; a time when colour is often short in the rock garden.

A few nurseries list *Shortia*, attractive woodland plants from America and Japan, which are worth looking out for although they may take a time to establish. They prefer a well-drained, light soil with peat and they resent disturbance.

Soldanella is another genus worth looking out for. The safest place for these delicate little plants with their beautifully fringed, pendent flowers, is at the foot of a large rock on the cool, north-facing side. The buds form in autumn and must overwinter safely if they are to open in spring so watch out for slugs. Protection from winter damp with a sheet of glass will also help to promote survival but the ground around the plants should not be allowed to dry out or the flower buds will abort.

Remaining for a moment with the smaller plants that prefer an open situation although out of the direct sun we may consider saxifrages. Many of them like this kind of position; they can be planted on the north side of a rock or better still planted directly into the shady side of a lump of tufa. Many of the so-called Kabschia saxifrages are thus suited and they are easy to obtain and to grow, producing a very attractive show with their domes of white, pink or yellow flowers.

Another low, but this time spreading plant, is *Linnaea borealis*, which is the only species in its genus. It is named after the Swedish botanist Linnaeus, the father of botanical nomenclature. It soon forms a prostrate mat of round or oval leaves from which rise stems bearing two bell-shaped pink flowers. There is a variety from N. America (var. *americana*) which has larger flowers and leaves and is a darker pink. *L. borealis* is a shrubby carpeter as is *Polygala chamaebuxus*. The type plant of the latter has yellow and cream, pea-like flowers but there is a form known as 'Grandi-flora' or 'Purpurea' in which the yellow is replaced by purple resulting in a very striking plant. This species, in either colour form, has the great advantage of flowering over a very long period, indeed it may produce flowers in any month of the year.

There are many other dwarf shrubs that are suitable for shady areas. The Society has published a guide (*Dwarf Shrubs* by H. E. Bawden) which covers many of these and I refer the reader to its interesting pages for inspiration. I mention this book partly because it is very useful to have but also because it will get me out of the problem of having to choose among the dwarf rhododen-drons which, like primulas, are legion. Some will tolerate more exposure than others but all are useful by providing in turn shade for other plants.

North facing crevices in rocks or stone walls are worth exploiting. The classic plants to grow in such situations are ramondas and haberleas. *Ramonda myconi* and *R. nathaliae* are the first to try, followed by *Haberlea rhodopensis*. All like to have a cool root run with ample moisture but with their rosettes of hairy leaves vertical to prevent moisture gathering in the crowns. Another genus which prefers to grow on its side in this way is *Lewisia*. One somehow associates lewisias, with their often hot colours and fleshy leaves, with hot conditions, but they prefer a little light shade, away from the hot midday sun. An east facing crevice would suit them very well. I have already written about primulas, but it is worth mentioning that many, such as *P. marginata* also enjoy growing in shady crevices. One group of plants that really look splendid on shady walls are the ferns. These will mostly do well in a range of light conditions provided the soil is not too dry, but the wall shows them off to perfection.

One of my favourite plants for shady positions, and one which will tolerate quite dry conditions, is the cyclamen. These often have the reputation of being difficult plants which is far from the truth and is probably due to their often being acquired as dormant tubers which may well be dead on arrival. Much better to get some *fresh* seed and sow it at once. If it cannot be had fresh then soak it overnight in water before sowing. Patience is needed in raising these lovely plants from seed as it can take several years before a decent flowering size corm has been built up. The flowering season for the hardy cyclamen species can take you almost right through the year: *C. hederifolium* (syn. *neapolitanum*) in the autumn followed by *C. coum* in its various forms from December to March, *C. repandum* from March to May and *C. purpurascens* (syn. *europaeum*) in July and August.

I have not mentioned the hardy ground orchids which are marvellous for illuminating a shady corner, nor yet the Solomon's Seals (*Polygonatum* spp.) with their arching stems and hanging flowers. Many violas prefer light shade, often scrambling up through low shrubs. And what about the genera *Epimedium*, *Vancouveria*, *Jeffersonia*, *Hypsella* and *Asarum*? Don't forget that many of the predominantly sun-loving genera have the odd shade-loving plants such as *Phlox* and *Iris*. *Ranunculus*, *Synthyris*, *Omphalodes*, *Mertensia*, *Tiarella*; the list of plants for shady areas seems to be almost limitless and I have obviously only been able to scratch the surface. One of the excitements of alpine gardening is that one is constantly coming across new plants. The plants mentioned are on the whole easy to obtain and grow and by all means use them as a basis for a collection but visits to gardens and nurseries, and the reading of nursery catalogues and seed lists will soon provide many more ideas and challenges. The best gardens are always those that reflect the owner's taste rather than a prescribed list.

Alpine Pilgrimages

by Michael Upward

There are many facets to alpine gardening: you can heave large rocks about to recreate the Himalayas; potter with a miniature landscape in a trough; muddle about in your man-made moraine or enjoy the delights of the protected glass of your alpine house in bad weather, but for me one of the highlights each year is when I can cast aside the cares of office routine and the telephone and escape to favourite haunts in the mountains. Over the past twenty-five years or more I have been very privileged to be able to lead parties to various parts of the world or travel there on my own account and it is really a summary of my journeys that I offer to you as a temptation, if you like, to steer yourself from the garden to see how alpines grow in the wild.

The obvious place to start is Europe as this is still the nearest and comparatively the cheapest centre for our studies. I happily declare a preference, built up over the years, for Switzerland, but it does not mean to say that I have not enjoyed myself in other parts of the continent. I have said, in an article in the AGS *Bulletin* for June 1985 that I consider the best place to begin in Europe is in the Bernese Oberland, basing yourself in one of the many centres, particularly in the Lauterbrunnen Valley. It would be repetitious to go into more detail and I can merely recommend you to page 134 of Volume 53, and also another article on the area by the late Norman Woodward – *Bulletin* Volume 46, page 64. These two articles should cover the Bernese Oberland for you.

Although I like the grandeur of the scenery that can be viewed from the top of the Schilthorn or beneath the Jungfrau or across from the north face of the Eiger, I still have a love for the Val d'Anniviers, which is a forked valley in the south of the Valais. You catch the train from Geneva to Sierre and then take the Postbus, or reserve a coach if you are in a party, up the twisting road to St Luc which although it is at 6000′ (1800m) or so has a commanding view of the valley and is a good centre. I first went there in 1962 with one of the very first parties I led. The walks from St Luc are many and varied and since we first went a road has been built up to the Weisshorn Hotel. On the last occasion I was there Professor Pontecorvo and I made our way eastwards to try to find the westernmost location in Switzerland of *Eritrichium nanum*, a plant that some travellers to the Alps consider essential to see to complete their holiday. It does not have that much of an allure for me, but is nevertheless an interesting goal to set as an objective to any tour. St Luc is now blessed with a chair lift towards the Bella Torla, a form of transport that does not endear itself to everybody, and indeed on the one and only occasion that I used it caused the whole circle to stop because the straps of my haversack entangled and I was suspended from my seat in a somewhat undignified manner. However, these are small inconveniences when the chair lifts whisk you to higher pastures.

The nature of the alpines at St Luc is fairly general. You have, of course, gentians abounding in the pastures, including the tall *Gentiana purpurea*; in fact my family and I have found it in flower in August and alongside the woodland paths in that same spot we remember seeing *Parnassia palustris*, the so called Grass of Parnassus, which is nowhere near being a grass botanically as it has its own family of *Parnassaceae*, having been booted out of its former family of *Saxifragaceae* by modern botanists. The higher flora above St Luc, which lies on a ledge to the north of the valley, is mainly of meadow plants and offers a good introduction to the beginner. The usual method of walking in the mountains where there are mechanical conveyances is to take whatever transport is offered up and walk down, an elementary lesson learnt very early on in our plant hunting careers.

The Bella Torla is a tall peak to the north of St Luc, and in my youth I did walk up it but truthfully cannot remember anything remarkable that we saw on the way, apart from the meadow androsaces, helianthemums, gentians, *Geum montanum* and the like. One very memorable, if unspectacular plant was a *Euphrasia* sp. of which I note there are 46 species, but which we gaily called *E.officinalis*, the Eyebright. It was interesting to see that it is still used in the treatment of eye ailments in modern times. Another plant that is memorable, also not very distinctive, was Cudweed, probably *Gnaphalium sylvaticum*, and the memory of the incredulous words of one member of the party ring in my ears to this day when I confessed that I had never heard of Cudweed in my life. I must be honest and say that I still do not think it is a very attractive plant, but I shall always remember it! We spent some time enjoying the buses in the valley, which are very efficient, and enable you to spend a good day away from the village. One branch of the valley to the south leads to Zinal, which is an unprepossessing village, mainly, I suspect, serving as a winter resort because there is a cable car taking you up above the village on to a very cold north facing slope, but the other branch of the valley leads to the very pretty, wooden houses of Grimentz and beyond to the Moiry Dam. If you are sufficient in number and can persuade the Postbus driver, he will take you, with some prior arrangement, to the top of the dam which is quite spectacular, but botanically unrewarding. However, on a late occasion in the early 1970s my family and I motored beyond the dam, alongside the lake and found, in late July or early August, *Campanula cenisia*. It was quite exciting.

If we stay in Switzerland and just go a little to the east we come across Saas Fee and Zermatt which are just a little too sophisticated for some people, but nevertheless they both guarantee good quality hotels and comfort and hot water on your return from the mountains. Zermatt has both cable cars and mountain railway – the latter to the Gornergrat, where, if you peer over the railings at the station exit, huge clumps of *Eritrichium nanum* can be seen hanging from the cliff seemingly with no visible means of support. Apart from the scenic views, particularly of the Matterhorn, there is little of botanical value unless you return to one of the lower stations, and walk back through the woods where, if the local populace has not picked them, you should find *Aquilegia alpina*. The only reason we know it grows in this area is because we saw bunches being carried!

The ambitious can take the cable car almost to the Theoduhl Pass and then ski over to Cervinia in Italy, but if you want to see plants then take a return to Schwarzsee and turn right towards the Matterhorn where, after a short while, *E. nanum* can be seen growing in the turf. Pressing on towards the Hornli Hut the turf gives way to scree where *Saxifraga oppositifolia* and *S. biflora* grow together, occasionally producing the hybrid between the two. Further down *Campanula cenisia* can be seen. If you feel you are deserving of a reward, then the cafe at Schwarzsee has the most delicious cream and strawberry concoctions to eat with your afternoon tea.

For those who enjoy or prefer camping, there is an excellent site at St Niklaus, the point beyond which you cannot take your car. However, it is a trifle busy and we prefer to camp at Saas Grund on the site at the bottom of the Kapellen Weg, which leads up to Saas Fee. There is also more modest hotel accommodation at Saas Almagell, for Saas Fee is a trifle up-market. We will never forget our first visit to Saas Fee with a party that commandeered the lounge for botanical study after dinner, to the undisguised fury of three English dames who had placed their knitting strategically to give the impression that the entire room was occupied by them. We discovered, when we made friends, that they journeyed each year to Switzerland to purchase their underwear! As ever, we digress.

Beyond Saas Grund lies Saas Almagell and the Monte Moro Dam, the construction of which we observed years ago, but whose banks are now clothed with alpines, notably *Campanula cenisia* and *Epilobium fleischeri*. Both these flower later in the season, that is the end of July and August. Above Saas Almagel is the Almagellertal, in which it is reputed that all endemics to the area grow. It is reached either by hard slog from the village or by taking a cable car obliquely to the south and walking back. On balance we thought the walk might be quicker! *E. nanum* abounds in this valley as it does beneath the cable car at Saas Fee. Obviously there are other delights in the area, such as *Androsace vandellii* at Saas Fee, but the Eritrichium does seem to dominate.

Moving further east in Switzerland to the Grisons area, a good base is Arosa. It can be reached by train from Zurich, changing at Chur, where the mountain railway line starts off along the streets and twists and turns up the valley to Arosa. The town is perched on a steep slope so that no matter where you stay you have to walk up either at the beginning or end of the day! However, transport is available, with cable cars up to both the Weisshorn and the Rothorn, although the latter seems to operate only later in the season. Several journeys can be made to the Weisshorn, for there are many permutations for walking back down. At the top grow *Androsace helvetica* and *A. alpina*, with the hybrid *A.* x *heerii* being fairly common nearby. One walk back is down the way of the cable car, with many primulas, gentians and pulsatillas, particularly *P. vernalis*, the loveliest of them all, and the other is towards the Carmenna pass, where some excellent forms of *Viola calcarata* can be observed. Turning left at Carmenna, back to Arosa, through damp alpine meadows, several species of *Soldanella* can be found. At the pass itself, a small but well-coloured form of *Primula auricula* can be found in the scree.

Below Arosa, in the Isel meadows in sparse woodland, *Cypripedium calceolus* enjoys the dappled sunshine. Also in the area can be found *Atragene alpina; Primula auricula balbisii;* the Moonwort, *Botrychium lunulatum; Gentiana punctata* and *G. lutea; Ranunculus aconitifolius* and *Anemone narcissiflora.* All in all, quite a rich flora. When I first went to Arosa it was for two weeks and I could not wait to leave; the next time it was for seven days and we could have stayed fourteen!

Not far away to the south is the Engadine, with Pontresina a good centre. Here the primulas dominate, with sufficient subtlety in their differences to tease the identifier. Some would declare this their favourite alpine haunt, but for me it has a harshness that I found to be uncomfortable. *E. nanum* is here again and the *Ranunculus glacialis* at the top of the Piz Palu are considered to be the best forms. This is an excellent area, if on the expensive side for accommodation. One particular walk remains vivid – by rack railway to Muottas Muragl and then along the path to Chamanna Segantini, where a red flag with a white cross indicates liquid refreshment; up till then the walk was unremarkable, but suitably refreshed and possibly with improved vision the descent produced *E. nanum, Androsace helvetica* and *Saxifraga oppositifolia* all within inches of each other.

I had not until recently travelled any further east, but there are many centres in Austria, Obergurgl for instance, that make good centres for alpines. We took a cheap package holiday in the autumn, not knowing at which resort we would be deposited, but landing at St. Wolfgang, which even in late September, early October had some items of interest in addition to evidence of earlier floral attractions. Leaves of *Helleborus niger* and *Hepatica nobilis* were abundant in the woods on the lower slopes, giving a hint of spring beauty, but we found *Cyclamen purpurascens, Gentiana asclepiadea, G. verna* and *G. ciliata* along with *Gentianella germanica* all in flower, with a few aconites, *Campanula pusilla, C. rotundifolia, Parnassia palustris,* colchicums, rampions, knapweeds and Scabious. Obviously the area is very rich, particularly the limestone lump of the Schafberg, at 1782m (5588ft), which is easily reached by an antique rack railway with many permutations of the walks that can be taken down its slopes. St. Wolfgang would be unpleasantly crowded in the high season, but was virtually deserted in the autumn. Hotels and bed and breakfast establishments were abundant.

Even further east lies Yugoslavia, with Mt Triglav an excellent goal for the intrepid flower hunter. Greece and the Balkans are also unknown territories to the writer, but both have first-class plants with articles for reference in the *Bulletin*. Mt Olympus in Greece has a specialised flora of its own and should be included in a Greek tour if at all possible. The difficult-to-cultivate *Jankaea heldreichii* is but one of the goals for this mountain. Turkey has the aura of adventure about it and the Society has organised tours there and plans to continue doing so. The eastern Mediterranean islands, Cyprus, Crete, Rhodes and Corfu are splendid for bulbs and orchids and are best visited early or late in the year for the benefits of cooler weather combined with more flowers: March/April and September/October are ideal; at the latter time the autumn-flowering crocuses and colchicums can be found.

Italy has several areas of interest to the alpine flower lover. The Dolomites are, of course, renowned, with many centres that offer rich floras. Our first ever trip to the mountains centred on a small village north of Misurina, itself north of Cortina d'Ampezzo and from the hotel we walked straight into lush pastures and in the limestone rock faces found *Physoplexis comosus* (syn. *Phyteuma comosum*) and *Rhodothamnus chamaecistus*, whilst in the low-growing scrub, hundreds of *Cypripedium calceolus* were growing. A visit to the Passo Pordoi led us along the Bindelweg, where Reginald Farrer himself had walked and found – yet again – *Eritrichium nanum*. Along the Great Dolomite Road children were selling *Lilium croceum* plucked from the woods, a habit we pray has ceased.

West of Pordoi are such places as Corvara and Madonna di Campiglio which offer pleasant walks in green pastures with helpful cable cars to the heights. Cervinia lies to the south of the Matterhorn, just into Italy and is good for a late holiday – in August we found *Campanula cenisia, Gentiana brachyphylla* and *Androsace alpina* in full flower on the higher screes.

Back down the valley from Cervinia is Aosta, a busy junction since Roman times and worth exploring for its historical antiquities, but in June/July it can be hot, sticky and dusty and less than congenial and so is best avoided – passing on further south to the

Gran Paradiso, an area rich in different alpine goodies.

And so to France – for the orchid-lovers there are areas in the lowlands that are rich with many species – the Dordogne and the Auvergne are such. The Alpes Maritimes are best visited in late May, early June, for *Primula allionii*, but it is the Savoy Alps that offer the real grandeur along with several suitable centres handy for the floral delights. We have stayed at La Grave, where the main disadvantage is the heavy lorry traffic *en route* to Italy. It may thus be better to stay in one of the villages above the town and a few years ago the Society's tour stayed at Les Hieres in a small hotel at the end of a muddy road but in full view of La Meije Glacier and with excellent French cuisine. The plants in the area are richly varied: one fortnight there in the late 1960's started off with pinks and blues and after a rainless twelve days finished with the yellow-brown hues in the meadows. All the usual 'cow-fodder' plants can be found, alongside *Lilium martagon, Aquilegia alpina, Atragene alpina* – all within a short walking distance of the village. A strenuous walk to Lac Noir on the Plateau de Paris will reward you with *Eritrichium nanum*, as will also the steep climb to Lac Chancel, but within 60 minutes of Lautaret, just beneath the Pic de Combeynot, *E. nanum* can be found with ease. Lautaret itself is a centre, but I cannot give a report on the only hotel in the village; it might well be noisy. On the road to Besançon are several stands of *Campanula alpestris*, formerly *C. allionii*, with its large upturned bells, and all down the slopes from the Col du Galibier, masses of the Elder Flowered Orchid, *Dactylorhiza sambucina*, can be found in both its red and yellow forms. In the screes and rocks at the top of the Col – to the east – are several interesting treasures: *Androsace helvetica, Saxifraga oppositifolia, S. biflora* and several intermediate forms, together with *Linaria alpina* and a mass, such as I have never seen before, of *Geum reptans*.

From the La Grave/Lautaret area you can travel to Briançon and up to the Col d'Izoard, which is approached from the west through pine trees that gradually thin out to nothing and the eventual total barrenness of its eastern side. I have never seen such a sudden contrast. If *Berardia subacaulis* was a more beautiful plant it would be sought after with the same fervour as, say, *Eritrichium* or *Androsace*, for it is even rarer than these. It can be found on the Col d'Izoard along with *Petrocallis pyrenaica*. A better display of the latter can be found on the Col de l'Iséran, which leads to the Val d'Isere, a popular and expensive skiing area. This is all within striking distance of Lanslebourg, a town well provided with hostelries, from which you can also reach the Mont Cenis area, another rich hunting ground for alpines.

Further south in France lie the Pyrenees. Our journey there was confined to one autumn visit many years ago, but it left indelible memories of the rich flora, for even at that time of year we found masses still in flower – even primulas and violas, but of course the main attraction was colchicum which we found in the form of *C. autumnale* 'Album'. Gavarnie is the mecca for plant hunters as well as pilgrims from Lourdes, so it is well to get above the village early in the morning where the walk towards the Cirque will reveal ramondas and androsaces, whilst the walls of the valleys lower down are clothed with the arching sprays of *Saxifraga longifolia*, a spectacular sight at flowering time. The gentian peculiar to the area is *G. pyrenaica*, a darker blue than most, but easily found along the French side at Andorra and Font Romeu. The Spanish side is attractive too, but somewhat drier later in the season; Espot in the west has been a tour centre, with a long list of plants found in June.

We have not travelled further south into Spain or Portugal, as to see the narcissi at their best requires a journey early in the year, say February to May, when it has not been possible. Southern Spain is worth a visit if only to see *Viola cazorlensis* by the roadside. More advice can be obtained for this area by reference to the *Bulletin* indexes or, if you are a Member, from the Panel of Experts.

Sardinia is one Mediterranean island that we have visited several times. When the flora of Sardinia is mentioned it seems to provoke the comment that the flowers of Corsica are better. Having now travelled to both, I would venture to suggest that the only point on which Corsica scores more is the French cuisine. Sardinia is largely unspoiled, apart from the over-developed Costa Smeralda and other parts of the northern coastline, with visitors still looked upon as curiosities by the local population. The most favourable time to go is early May, when the orchids are at their best; after this the herbage begins to turn brown and sere. There are several mountains to explore and we have experience of three: Monte Limbara, Monte Albo and Supramonte di Oliena. The latter was described as 'quasi-lunare' in an Italian guide book, which certainly was apt for the moonscape look of the mountain top in which it appeared that nothing grew. However, we continued to translate the guide book and eventually discovered what we were looking for: *Paeonia russii* – hardly an alpine, but certainly a mountain plant.

On Monte Albo, a limestone block on the east coast south of Olbia, we were in a small party and played leapfrog with the cars which enabled the less agile to see the lime-loving plants of the area. There were many orchids along the mountain roadside: *Aceras anthropophorum*, the Man Orchid; *Barlia robertiana*, the Giant Orchid, which can be up to 80cm; *Limodorum abortivum*, the pale purple chlorophyll-free flower spikes usually found in the edges of woodland and again this can get as tall as 80cm. Ophrys abounded: *O. tenthredinifera*, the Sawfly Orchid with its distinctive pinkish flowers with green veining; *O. fusca*, which has many variations and sub-species, but basically the sepals are green to yellow, with green or yellowish or light brown petals and a dark brown lip; *O. lutea*, which as its name suggests is basically yellow and *O. sphegodes*, the Early Spider Orchid, again with several sub-species.

The effect of Monte Limbara, to the west of Olbia, is totally ruined by the presence of radar antennae at its peak – visible from all around and oppressive and ugly once the peak is reached, as it so happens very easily by a tarmac road. However, the mountain was botanically very rewarding and many treasures were found, including a magnificent gully of *Cyclamen repandum*. The Tongue Orchid, *Serapias lingua*, together with *S. cordigera* and their intermediates were abundant on the lower slopes. We did not trace *Morisia monanthos*, although it was reputed to be not far away.

There are many more plants to be found, but space and memory cannot accommodate them all. I do however, remember well the sight of *Gladiolus segetum* as a weed in the cornfields and *Convolvulus althaeoides* as a roadside inhabitant. *Ornithogalum arabicum* had long fascinated me and it was exciting to find it growing in the rocks at Capo Testa not far from healthy clumps of armeria growing in pure sand. We have had difficulty in establishing *Arenaria balearica* on the shady peat blocks in our garden, but here we found it in both shade and sun clinging to the rocks. *Frankenia laevis* was hugging the ground, producing a profusion of its pink flowers and in the rocks again were the large strap-shaped leaves and white flowers of *Pancratium illyricum*. All in all Sardinia is a paradise for plants and worth a visit for the keen plantsman.

Corsica seemed a mite more sophisticated and in truth we appeared to find less to excite us than perhaps one should. Our base was in the centre not far from Corte, and we were able to explore several of the valleys running from east to west, which were scenically outstanding. The Gorge de Restonica is a must and here was found *Helleborus corsicus* together with *Crocus corsicus* in early May. Otherwise most of the flora was a repeat of Sardinia, with perhaps the added excitement of *Cyclamen repandum* 'Album' seen along one roadside.

For a really exotic, exciting and strenuous plant-hunting adventure the Himalayas are more open than they have ever been – even Tibet is approachable from Nepal now, whereas before you had to journey there via Peking and then through Yunnan. Nevertheless excitement should not reach fever-pitch just yet, for the Chinese authorities are not yet happy to allow any old tourist to go plant hunting in the deeper areas of their country and still operate considerable controls on your travels there.

The Society in 1983 organised its first expedition – to Sikkim in the Eastern Himalaya, whither in fact any traveller, with the required finance and stamina can travel. A full account of this expedition and the flora encountered is to be found in the September 1984 issue of the *Bulletin*.

There is no need to go to such strenuous lengths to see the Himalayan flora, for one thing the western end is much drier and for another there are well-organised holiday walks offered by reputable travel companies and led by knowledgeable plantsmen. You would need a minimum of three weeks to do any such tour justice and if you could manage six weeks, as some members of the Society have, then a private journey can be arranged. This short two paragraph mention of a great mountain chain is not intended to be dismissive – no article could do justice to the floral beauties and so it must be regarded as a lead-in to a very rich area.

Our final area for alpine pilgrimages is North America. With the advent of the American Rock Garden Society's Interim International Conferences now a permanent feature in our calendars, albeit once in ten years, more members have been encouraged to travel across the Atlantic. Whereas the fare across seems a stumbling block, it has become comparatively cheaper and living and travelling in the United States has become relatively cheap. Canada is not so cheap as the exchange rate is harsher. There are some incredible fly-drive bargains with ridiculously cheap car hire rates and petrol is less expensive than in Britain.

Where to go in America? The Rockies are an obvious choice, with a journey that could extend from British Columbia through Alberta and into Montana, Wyoming, Colorado and almost to Mexico. The West Coast in Washington and Oregon offers areas of equal interest – the Olympic Mountains, the Cascades, the Wenatchees, with the series of extinct and not so extinct volcanic peaks all the way down to Mt Shasta in California. In this comparatively short article it is not possible to cover this vastly rich area, so we refer you to an excellent publication produced by the American Rock Garden Society as the Conference Report in 1986: 'Rocky Mountain Alpines' – it leads you through the entire range and is generously illustrated. It is available from AGS Publications Ltd. When we went we took with us the series of articles written by Eric Hilton in the AGS *Bulletin* from 1977 onwards, and these virtually led us by hand to the various locations.

Photographing Alpines

by Phil Phillips

This chapter has been written for the alpine gardener who is chiefly interested in plants and who may wish to take better than average pictures; it was not written for the expert photographer. I have endeavoured to avoid technical details wherever possible, but to take good pictures it is necessary to understand some of the principles involved.

While it has been assumed that the photographer is operating in the wild, many of the aspects discussed apply equally to photography in the garden, the greenhouse, or on the show bench. It has also been assumed that the photographer is using colour films.

My aim is to produce good pictures that are pleasing to the eye and, at the same time, botanically accurate. They should impart to the viewer the maximum amount of information about the subject that it is possible to convey on film. One picture is seldom sufficient to do this for a single plant; therefore I suggest a sequence of three – the habitat, the plant and a close-up.

A good photograph should show the subject – carefully framed, sharply defined, adequately and sometimes dramatically illuminated, and properly exposed. When these four requirements are satisfied, a better than adequate picture will result.

Recommended equipment

The type and quantity of equipment that you take on your holiday or photographic expedition can be directly proportional to the size of your bank balance and the weight you are prepared to carry. A first class camera should be used; however, expensive and elaborate equipment is not necessary as it is the photographer who creates the picture.

The following are recommended as essential items for plant photography:

A single-lens-reflex (SLR) camera. The important feature of an SLR camera is that the image produced by the lens is the one that the photographer sees in the viewfinder, and is also the one that is recorded on the film. This is crucial when photographing objects that are close to the camera. Using a SLR camera the photographer has no difficulty in framing the subject and finds that parallax errors are non-existent. Accurate focussing is made easy and depth of field decisions greatly facilitated. Lenses of various focal lengths may be fitted. The majority of modern SLR cameras sold for use by the amateur are fitted with a through-the lens (TTL) metering system – more about this later. Many SLR cameras have interchangeable viewing screens, e.g. split image, Fresnel field, matte etc. – ask to try them all and choose the one that suits you best.

A macro lens. A macro lens will focus from infinity down to a reproduction ratio of 1:2, which is half life size on the slide or negative. A macro lens can be used for the habitat, the plant, and for most close-ups without the bother of adding extension rings or tubes.

A right-angle viewing attachment. This permits viewing from "waist-level" and is invaluable when photographing small plants, avoiding the inconvenience of lying prone on the ground. Most can be rotated through 360 degrees which allows the camera to be placed in any position. The model that I use incorporates a variable correction lens that can be adjusted to suit the photographers' eyes and spectacles. It also presents the viewer with an unreversed image, i.e. the plant is the right way up.

A rigid tripod. Many otherwise excellent pictures are spoilt because of camera shake. A tripod should be used so that the camera is as still as possible, and this is particularly important for close-up photography when using natural light. Use a tripod that is rigid and is not too heavy to carry! For small plants the tripod should open out completely so that the head is almost at ground level.

A cable release. For use when the camera is mounted on a tripod (I *always* use a tripod) – for taking long exposures – or when the camera is fitted with a long focus lens.

Photographing the habitat

The purpose of the habitat picture is to show as comprehensively as possible the surroundings in which the plant is growing. Unless the plant is extremely small, it should be visible in the picture frame and the shot should establish the scale of the habitat in relation to the size of the plant.

Habitats often mean landscapes and with thought and care they can often be made into attractive pictures. For good landscapes, lighting is extremely important, and is influenced by a number of factors, e.g. the weather and the time of day. Unfortunately the plant hunter must often take his picture as and when a plant is found, and is unable to wait until the light is just right.

A landscape lit from behind the camera should reproduce the habitat faithfully, but with a flat and often uninteresting appearance. This is accentuated if the scene is photographed during the middle of the day. Low-angle lighting in early morning and late afternoon is much 'warmer' and conveys a three dimensional form to your picture, which will now contain both light and shade. Side light also introduces a little modelling giving the subject shape and depth. With three-quarter and full back lighting the landscape becomes dramatic, turning what was a flat picture into something more exciting. Whilst it is not possible to move the subject or the sun, it is usually possible to move the camera so as to take advantage of these different effects.

Unless your lens is deeply recessed into its mounting, always use a lens hood, particularly for back- and side-lit subjects. The lens hood should be one designed for the focal length of the lens being used. For back-lit subjects the lens must be shielded against direct light to avoid flare. Hold your hand, a book or similar above and slightly in front of the lens hood, and of course out of the picture, and cast a shadow on the lens.

Often when you wish the sun to shine it will not. Don't despair, as adequate landscapes can be obtained with a continuous cloud cover which often provides a soft diffuse light. It can, however, produce a picture with a bluish cast which may be corrected with a filter. Heavy cloud can produce dramatic effects; look for the positive factors and try to discount the negative ones.

A wide-angle lens can sometimes be helpful for associating plants with their habitats because foreground subjects (the plants) appear larger and distant objects further away. It is also helpful when working in a confined space (a 100m cliff immediately behind one, for example) as it certainly extends perspective. Do not overdo this, otherwise a distorted picture devoid of scale will result. I find a 35mm lens quite satisfactory for this purpose. The wide-angle lens also has the advantage of giving a greater depth of field for a given aperture than a standard lens and if well stopped down (small aperture, which is equivalent to a large 'f' number) it will produce a picture with both the foreground (including the plant) and distant objects in focus. Unfortunately distant objects include not just snow-capped mountains and alpine chalets but also telegraph wires and cable-car towers so be careful when using a wide-angle lens to ensure that everything in the frame is required in the final picture.

Much is written about filters for landscapes. I seldom use them. It is recommended by some writers that an ultra-violet ('Skylight') filter is left permanently on the camera. I find that it makes very little difference to the picture, but it does protect the lens. Occasionally I use a polarizing filter which can increase the contrast between clouds and sky; it is also useful for reducing reflections on water when photographing aquatic plants.

Whilst I have suggested that the habitat picture should be as exciting as possible, do not lose sight of the prime objective, which is to show, as faithfully as possible, the plant and the surroundings in which it grows.

Photographing the whole plant

While the composition of all photographs is important, the careful framing of the plant is essential if the desired impact is to be made. This does not mean that the subject must always be in the centre of the frame. Edges and borders of the frame should be as free as possible from superfluous and distracting material. Many otherwise presentable pictures are ruined by a tangle of grass or twigs either around, behind, or even in front of the subject. A limited amount of "gardening" is sometimes necessary and is usually acceptable providing it is reduced to a minimum. The exceptions occur when photographing rare plants, which should never be disturbed. The well-being of the plant rather than one's own ego as a photograher should be uppermost in the mind at such times. At all events the aim should be to produce a photograph which combines botanical accuracy with attractive presentation.

Do not automatically photograph the first specimen of a particular species that you find, be selective, and whenever possible photograph good representative plants. It is pointless to photograph poor specimens unless they are rare and as such the only ones likely to be seen. Even then there are often better plants available if only you take the trouble to look. This may take time and can prove to be a problem if you are with a party!

Whenever possible ensure that any visible features of the plant necessary for its identification are clearly shown, even if this means taking more than one picture. The close-up, which is dealt with in the next section, is often useful for this purpose. Back lighting is excellent for showing hairs and spines to good effect and, as a bonus sunlight passing through translucent petals can add sparkle to an otherwise ordinary picture. With front-lit subjects, make sure that you or your equipment do not cast a shadow into the picture area.

Whilst the eye can cope with extreme contrasts between light and dark areas, colour films are unable to do so. A plant with white or pastel flowers and dark green leaves (even without shadows) will present a problem if you attempt to photograph it in strong direct sunlight. In this case try to light your subject with indirect or diffuse lighting; wait for a cloud to obscure the sun, use a diffuser, or cast a shadow if the plant is not too large.

Assuming that the camera used is a 35mm and not one with a square picture format, if the plant is taller than it is wide the camera should be turned through 90 degrees, producing a vertical rather than a horizontal picture. A tall thin plant set in a horizontal frame is quite acceptable for the habitat shot but not for the plant picture itself.

Photographing plants in the open is seldom simple, in fact it can be positively difficult in windy conditions. Frequently the plant or parts of it will be moving, sometimes violently, and unless the movement is restricted the result will be a blurred subject on the exposed film. Flash is the obvious way of overcoming this problem but some photographers, myself included, prefer to use natural light whenever possible. An alternative to flash is the use of fast shutter speeds in order to arrest the movement but this can result in depth of field problems which are discussed later.

It is therefore necessary to keep the subject as still as possible. A windbreak is all I can suggest and I use one frequently. My wife is often crouched on the windward side of the plant holding an outstretched coat to break the force of the wind. A transparent plastic sheet stretched between two stakes driven into the ground can also be effective, and is very light to carry. The windbreak technique only works if the plants are not too large, but if they are, you must exercise patience, wait for a lull or come back another day if you are able. Needless to say, take care to ensure that the windbreak is kept out of the picture frame.

Photographing close-ups

Close-up or supplementary lenses represent the cheapest and, with fixed lens cameras, the only solution to close-up photography. Their use does not lead to an increase in exposure factors, as is the case when a macro-lens or an extension tube is used. However, although close-up lenses can provide reasonable central sharpness depending on the lens to which they are attached, they are not the ideal solution for our needs so are not considered further.

For practical purposes I find that a 55mm macro-lens is ideally suited for the close-up photography of flowers and foliage. It is capable of focussing continuously from infinity down to a reproduction ratio of 1:2 (half life size), and then down to 1:1 (life size) with the introduction of an extension tube. Longer focal length macro-lenses are available and with these the camera will be further away from the subject for a given reproduction ratio thus making the lighting of the subject easier. The disadvantages are that the longer lens is heavier and camera shake is magnified. With a longer focal length lens depth of field is shallower at a fixed distance from the subject but is about the same for a given reproduction ratio.

Many of the factors discussed earlier must be taken into account when engaged in close-up photography, in particular, depth of field (the zone in front and behind the point on which the camera is focussed within which the subject appears sharply defined). The camera has a much more limited depth of field than that experienced by the eyes, and it is when taking close-ups that this becomes most noticeable.

Depth of field is affected by: –

1. The focal length of the lens – the longer the focal length the shallower the depth of field.
2. The distance between the point on which the lens is focussed and the camera itself – the shorter the distance the shallower the depth of field.

3. The size of the aperture of the lens iris – the smaller the aperture (i.e. the greater the 'f' number) the greater the depth of field.

Close-up pictures are obtained by placing the camera closer to the subject and at the same time increasing the distance between the lens and film. This increase in distance is achieved by extending the macro-lens itself and, when necessary, inserting the extension tube between the lens and the camera. As the distance is increased (i.e. the closer the lens is to the subject) so the exposure must be increased. With a reproduction ratio of 1:2 the exposure factor is approximately × 2, e.g. f16 increased to f11 or 1/30sec increased to 1/15sec. For a ratio of 1:1 (life size) the exposure factor is approximately × 4, e.g. f16 increased to f8 or 1/30sec increased to 1/8sec. As all modern SLR cameras have TTL (through the lens) metering the photographer need not worry about calculating exposure factors, the camera will perform this function.

It will be seen that photographing close-ups using natural light will require longer exposures as the smaller aperture used to increase the depth of field will necessitate correspondingly slower shutter speeds.

Any movement of either camera or subject is magnified the closer they are to each other which, coupled with the longer exposure, makes it doubly important to restrict the movement of both to a minimum. In addition to the windbreak already discussed a twig or similar object propped against the subject can sometimes help to keep it still. Always take care to ensure such supports are outside the camera frame. As far as the camera is concerned, a rigid tripod will certainly much reduce shake.

From my own experience it is usually possible to obtain good close-ups with the technique that I have described even when operating in natural light and using a slow film (say ASA 25 or 64). I must add, however, that I am greatly helped by the assistance of my wife and that many of my pictures are only obtained by exercising considerable patience.

It is possible to mitigate some of the problems that I have discussed by using faster films, which are improving every year, or by using flash. The latter is consistently used by many expert plant photographers with excellent results and while I prefer to use natural light I must admit that I prefer a picture taken with flash to no picture at all. The use of flash is dealt with later in this chapter.

For close-ups, focussing is critical, there being very little room for error. It is useful to know that the zone of sharpness is greater beyond the point on which the lens is focussed than in front of that point; approximately 2:1. Most SLR cameras have a depth of field preview button which allows the photographer to view the subject with the lens stopped down to whatever 'f' value is chosen for the exposure. This is valuable, as virtually all modern lenses operate at full aperture until the moment the shutter release is pressed in order to allow the maximum of light to enter the camera and thus the brightest possible image to be seen while the picture is being composed. While it is important to get as much as possible of the background in focus, it is even more necessary that the foreground is sharp, since the eye naturally goes first to this part of the photograph. Experience will soon allow the photographer to estimate depth of field and to ensure that, where appropriate, the subject is sharp but the background is blurred. This is known as selective focus and is ideal for isolating a subject from a distracting background, thus gaining maximum impact. Eliminate, where possible, bright objects such as light coloured stones or flowers from the background, which should be as free from strong contrasts as possible.

The points previously made that relate to vertical and horizontal formats – framing, avoiding distracting borders and edges, etc. – should all be observed when taking close-ups. In order to remove unwanted stems and foliage it is sometimes possible to tie or hold them back out of the way.

To summarize: –

1.   Stop down to bring your subject into focus but leave the background, where it is not wanted, out of focus and blurred.

2.   Keep the camera and plant as still as possible since exposure times will usually have to be long.

3.   If at first you don't succeed, keep trying!

Exposure

Once the subject has been framed and brought into focus the photographer must determine the correct exposure to produce the required photograph.

Exposure for a film of given speed is influenced by the intensity of the light reaching the film and the time that this light is allowed to fall on it. These factors, light intensity and duration, are variable and can be controlled either by the photographer through the camera, or by the camera itself if it is so programmed. The intensity can be varied by altering the aperture of the lens iris and the duration by changing the shutter speed.

Until relatively recently exposures were determined either by the photographer using a separate hand-held exposure meter, or by following the film manufacturer's recommendations. These suggested values still provide a valid guide should your hand-held or TTL meter fail.

Most modern cameras sold for amateur use have their own built-in metering systems. SLR cameras are now fitted with some form of through-the-lens (TTL) system using light sensitive cells situated inside the camera to measure the intensity of light entering the lens. The measurement obtained is displayed so as to allow the photographer to determine aperture and speed and thus the required exposure. In addition, many cameras today are pro-grammed to make the choice automatically, leaving the photo-grapher little to do! But beware! The exposure determined by any metering system should be treated as a guide and whilst under the majority of conditions it will be an accurate indication of the correct exposure, under others it can be quite misleading. No metering system is infallible. Of course, if you purchase an auto-matic only camera then you will have no choice over exposure: a good reason for buying one with a manual override which will enable you to accept or reject the recommended exposure.

There are various systems of TTL metering used in cameras currently sold to amateurs:

1. Average integrated reading – excellent where the whole frame has more or less equal proportions of light and shade but not so good where an important though small part of the picture is strongly contrasted with the surrounding area. Good for 'average' pictures.
2. Centre weighted – measures the whole area but gives greater weight to the reading from the middle of the frame. This assumes that the most important part of the picture is in the centre, which is not always the case.
3. Multiple patterned – where the light is individually measured from a number of separate areas of the focussing screen and then 'analyzed' by the camera's microcomputer.
4. Spot – measures only the central portion of the frame. This allows the photographer, by focussing on different parts of the

eventual frame, to measure any part of the area as he would with a hand-held meter.

It is important to know which of these systems your camera uses so that you can interpret the exposure information it gives you.

Although few difficulties will be experienced when exposing for an 'average' picture, care must be taken when dealing with very light or dark subjects or those with a high degree of contrast. As a general guide, if the habitat is predominantly light (e.g. snow or limestone rocks) the lens should be opened one half a stop ('f' unit) or one whole stop – sometimes more – otherwise the darker portions, namely the plant being photographed, will be under-exposed. The limitations of the meter together with the narrow latitude of most colour films mean that for pictures containing high contrast, judgment must be exercised. Under- or over-exposure will cause loss of detail in the darker or lighter areas respectively, therefore, ultimately the exposure will be a compromise.

Some photographers prefer to use incident light readings, i.e. the light falling on the subject is measured as distinct from that reflected by it.

Exposure for back-lit subjects presents further problems. For near subjects that are not translucent, meter the sunny side and then open by one stop before shooting from the shady side. Alternatively, move in close to the subject so that it fills the frame, take your meter reading from that position, and then step back and take your picture. For translucent subjects use your meter as the main indicator. For landscapes there is no hard and fast rule; each situation will be different.

It is recommended that you experiment by 'bracketing' exposures, i.e. taking several identical pictures of the same subject at slightly different exposure settings. In the end it is experience that will count; know your equipment, know your film, and know what sort of picture you require.

Films and colour

For the purpose of this article only colour films have been considered. They may be divided into two categories: –

1. Colour negative films – when processed give a negative image of the subject from which a positive print can be made.

2. Colour reversal film – which gives colour transparencies for direct viewing.

Prints may be obtained from transparencies, but although processing has improved considerably, they are inferior to those obtained from a colour negative film.

Transparencies, which are preferred for graphic reproduction (books, magazines, etc.), should be rather more dense than usual and with well saturated colour.

Colour negative film can be copied to produce transparencies if required.

Much has been written about the merits of various films – speed, grain, exposure latitude etc. My advice is to try a number and then select the fastest that will give you the results you require. Unfortunately the film of my choice is probably the slowest on the market! Once you have made your selection keep to it until a better film becomes available. Unless you need a different film for a special purpose do not flit from one to another.

As preferences for particular colour rendition are so subjective I do not propose to discuss the merits of particular films in this regard here, except to mention the problem that arises when photographing some blue flowers. Certain pigments reflect some of the red and infra-red light which then becomes mauve on the film. This phenomenon is accentuated by sunlight and it therefore helps to photograph these difficult blues in the shade. The use of flash has been recommended by some photographers in these circumstances.

Photographing with flash

As I have already indicated, I prefer the results produced by using natural light when photographing plants in the wild. Flash tends to give a dark and unnatural background, but this can sometimes be turned to advantage and used to isolate the subject from an unwanted background.

Flash can arrest plant movement, but only to a limited degree with SLR cameras, which are usually synchronised at a relatively slow speed.

Because of its powerful illumination in close proximity to the subject it is possible to stop down and gain extra depth of field – very useful for close-ups.

The use of flash to supplement natural light, normally referred to as 'fill-in-flash', can sometimes eliminate disquieting shadows and at the same time reduce extreme contrasts.

When photographing plants indoors, for example on the show bench, where natural light is often poor, flash is frequently a necessity. Used accurately, consistent results will ensue thus producing pictures of an even quality; a desirable factor when photographing in this environment.

Some modern flash units can operate in an automatic as well as a manual mode. In manual mode it is necessary to calculate the aperture from any given flash to subject distance by using a simple formula provided with the operating instructions. As these formulae are calculated assuming that the photographer is working under cover, it is advisable, for photographing in the field, to calculate your own table by running through a test film, bracketing exposures. A dedicated automatic flash unit will do the same, working in tandem with the camera's own light meter and shutting off the flash when sufficient exposure has been achieved. These dedicated flash units are simple to use, but do have their limitations, so make sure before purchasing one that it will operate within the parameters you require.

Another option for close-ups is the use of 'ring' flash. This consists, as the name suggests, of a ring-shaped flash unit attached to the front of the lens, which is synchronised with the shutter mechanism. It has the advantage of producing all-round illumination and thus avoiding the deep shadow which can be a problem with normal flash. It is used a lot by scientists for photographing objects, including plants and animals, where accurate recording of every detail of the subject is required.

Whatever kind of flash gun you purchase, read the manual carefully and then experiment with the different techniques described. One piece of ancillary equipment which can be very useful is a camera to flash extension lead. This will enable you to place the flash unit away from the camera, for example when one particular part of the picture area requires extra illumination.

Final points

1.   If you do not take photographs throughout the year, test your equipment before the season commences or before you go away on holiday. If you change any piece of equipment, test again.

2.   Make sure that the film speed is correctly set when loading the camera and keep a note of the film you are using and its speed.

3.   Make sure that your film is winding on. This is best done when

loading the film by turning the rewind lever until the film is fairly tightly wound onto the spool in the cassette and then winding on. The rewind lever should rotate as you do so. If it does not, open the camera and reload the film.

4.   Renew the batteries in your camera and flash at the beginning of each season. Take spare batteries with you.

5.   If you have a spare, hand-held light meter, take it with you. It can be used for difficult exposures and for checking your camera metering system from time to time.

Conclusions

Experiment with techniques, exposures, lighting etc. – it is the best way to improve. Do not be discouraged if some fail; develop those that are successful. Keep records of what you have done for future reference.

Some of the aspects discussed may seem rather involved to some readers, very elementary to others. You can make plant photography as simple or as complicated as you choose. Whatever you do, enjoy this fascinating and absorbing hobby which can bring great pleasure to you and to many others. My wife and I have enjoyed photographing alpines and other wild flowers for the past twenty years and we are still learning.

Alpine Bookshelf

by Michael Upward

The most frequent request from beginners is for a 'complete' book on alpines. This is a subject, remember, that includes both native species from the world over and cultivars raised for garden use. Generally speaking, the interests of Members fall into groups, which is helpful, as most growers eventually specialise, thus making the choice of books simpler. The request for one comprehensive volume will never be fulfilled, for in the following list are mentioned 69 books with probably thousands of pages, all told, of text and photographs.

Propagation

Still the best for general guidance after more than 30 years in print is, *The Propagation of Alpine Plants*, by Lawrence D. Hills (Faber & Faber 1950, now available as a reprint from Theophrastus Publishers, 545 Madison Avenue, New York (watch the AGS, RHS and SRGC book lists for this and other titles reprinted by this publisher). *Propagation of Alpine Plants* by J. K. Hulme is a handy booklet in the AGS Guide series.

General

The choice here depends on how deeply you wish to dive into references and your pocket. Good background works are the *RHS Dictionary of Gardening* (5 volumes, Oxford University Press) but not comprehensive on alpines, and the hideously expensive *Flora Europaea* (Cambridge University Press) for up-to-date nomenclature on European plants. *The English Rock Garden* by Reginald Farrer (2 volumes, T. C. & E. C. Jack 1918) is expensive in its original editions, but with its essential supplement, *Present Day Rock Gardening* by Sampson Clay, it is currently available as a reprint from Theophrastus. Coming down to more reasonable prices, *Collins Guide to Alpines* by Anna Griffith is now available in a cheap paperback form and is to be recommended. Still a useful guide for those requiring colour is *Alpines in Colour and Cultivation* by T. C. Mansfield (Collins 1942), long out of print, but still available from specialist secondhand booksellers. Currently in print and worthy of consideration is Ingwersen's *Manual of Alpine Plants* (1978) which has no illustrations, but comprises a descriptive list of alpines known and grown by that famous firm of nurserymen over the years.

I would modestly guide the real beginner towards my own small volume, *An Illustrated Guide to Alpines* (1983), in the Salamander series. This contains descriptions of only 150 plants, but it is well illustrated. *The Rock Gardener's Handbook* by Alan Titchmarsh (Croom Helm 1983) is now in paperback as well as hard cover and is a useful reference, with two others from the Ingwersen stable: *Alpine Garden Plants* (Blandford 1981), in either hard or soft cover, and *Alpines and Rock Plants* (Dent 1983) both by Will Ingwersen. The Bloom family of nurserymen has also made a notable contribution to alpine literature: *Alpines for Trouble-free Gardening* by Alan Bloom (Faber & Faber 1961) is out of print, but currently *Alpines for your Garden* (Floraprint 1980) is available. Adrian Bloom specialises in conifers and he has produced two slim, reasonably priced paperbacks: *Conifers* and *Alpines*, which are both excellent starters for the beginner and last, but not least, is the Society's own *Alpine Gardening* by Winton Harding, written especially as a beginners' guide.

Bulbs

This interest is well catered for: Brian Mathew is an acknowledged authority and has produced some classic offerings, both general and specific. *Dwarf Bulbs* (1973) and its companion *The Larger Bulbs* (1978), would be of interest. *The Iris* (1981) and *The Crocus* (1982) are two very thorough works, the latter superbly illustrated. All these are published by Batsford, as are his latest offerings in conjunction with Turhan Baytop, *The Bulbous Plants of Turkey* (1984) and *The Smaller Bulbs* (1987).

Pan Books have produced *The Bulb Book* by Martyn Rix and Roger Phillips, currently available in hard or soft back. The photographic study of the subject is outstanding, with details of the plants in close-up and in their native habitats. Over 800 species and cultivars are covered. *Bulbs* by Christopher Grey-Wilson and Brian Mathew (Collins 1981) has some first-class illustrations by Marjorie Blamey – it has recently been on special offer and represents quite a bargain. It would not be unkind to say that this is a good book which has not received the recognition it deserves. It has a section on orchids – not the easiest of plants to identify. If you want a more comprehensive orchid book, then try *Wild Orchids* by Paul and Jenne Davies and Anthony Huxley (Chatto and Windus 1983). It has some of the best colour reproductions I have ever seen and now accompanies me on my European travels, although not in my knapsack, where the lighter *Orchids of Britain and Europe* by Williams, Williams and Arlott (Collins 1978) travels instead, although I am still confused in my attempts at identification!

Specific Genera

One would be remiss not to mention the Society's specialist publications on *Cyclamen, Saxifrages, Lewisias, Daphnes, Androsaces* and the two Primula books: *Asiatic Primulas* and *Primulas of Europe and America.*

Recently published is *The Smaller Rhododendrons* by Peter Cox of Glendoick Gardens (Batsford 1985), a long-awaited and authoritative book. *Gentians* by Mary Bartlett (published in 1975 by Batsford, re-published by Alpha Books in 1981 in a larger format) deals with the genus competently, with some good photographs. For the keen enthusiast, *Gentians in the Garden* by G. H. Berry (Faber & Faber 1951) and *Gentians* by David Wilkie (Country Life 1936) are two collectors' items worthy of pursuit in the specialist booksellers' lists.

The Handbook of Cultivated Sedums by Ron Evans (Science Review 1983) has authority: *Saxifrages and Related Genera* by Fritz Kohlein (Batsford 1984), translated from the German by David Winstanley, is well illustrated. *Campanulas* by Clifford Crook (Country Life 1951) has still to be improved upon and remains the standard work, and has recently been reprinted. Likewise *The Dianthus* by Will Ingwersen (Collins 1949) – a small but interesting volume.

Specific Subjects

Again, the Society has produced *Alpines in Pots*, which covers alpine house cultivation; *Alpines in Sinks and Troughs* and *Dwarf Shrubs*. *Alpine House Culture for Amateurs* by Gwendolyn Anley (Country Life 1951) covers the subject well, but is difficult to obtain. The subject is, in any case, covered in *Collectors' Alpines* by Royton Heath (Collingridge 1964, but reprinted several times). This is an acknowledged reference book for those who have reached a stage or two beyond being a beginner. My first edition cost me four guineas – would that it was that price today! For rock garden construction there is a companion chapter in this Handbook, but if you wish to be more technical, then look for *Natural Rock Gardening* by B. H. B. Symons-Jeune (Country Life 1932). Years ago, the person who introduced me to the Society presented me with two small soft covered booklets by Capt. H. P. Leschallas entitled *The Small Alpine Garden*. They served me well in my early years and although now outdated still contain a few gems of wisdom and advice. They were printed and published some time before 1947 by the Society's then printers, Rush & Warwick of Bedford for the extravagant sum of 3/3d post free each.

The Peat Garden and its Plants by Alfred Evans (Dent 1974) is an outstanding reference book by an authority on the subject for those who garden on acid soil and it is beautifully illustrated. Conversely, *Alpines* by Lionel Bacon (David & Charles 1973) is written by an author who has gardened successfully on the chalk soil of Hampshire. *Alpines and Bog Plants* by Reginald Farrer (Arnold 1908) has been described as 'more valuable for its scarcity than the wisdom it contains'. Its modern counterpart is probably *The Damp Garden* by Beth Chatto (Dent 1982) but this book covers a wider field than just damp-loving alpines.

In the Field

For travelling abroad there is no shortage of references – all depending on your strength and depth of pocket. In my younger days I never travelled without Thompson's *Alpine Plants of Europe* (Routledge 1911), but not only has my copy become travel-worn, the book has become a collectors' item. Nowadays I arm myself with the following: *Mountain Flowers* by Anthony Huxley (Blandford 1967) but replaced by *The Alpine Flowers of Britain and Europe* by Christopher Grey-Wilson, illustrated by

Marjorie Blamey (Collins 1979); *Atlas de Poche de la Flore Suisse* by Edouard Thommen, the delight of this book being the 3,000 line drawings, albeit small scale, to which reference can be made; there is a companion volume, *Flore de la Suisse*, but it is bad enough struggling with English botanical descriptions, let alone French. I also find Collins *Pocket Guide to Wild Flowers* of value, for the illustrations are in colour groupings, which makes for simpler initial identification. For orchids we take the books already mentioned.

For home consumption, rather than to be conveyed on holiday, are a number of excellent volumes from the Oxford University Press by Oleg Polunin; *Flowers of Europe* (1969); *Flowers of South-west Europe* (1973); *Flowers of Greece and the Balkans* (1980). With Anthony Huxley, Oleg has also written *Flowers of the Mediterranean* (Chatto & Windus 1972), which is not too heavy for a knapsack and the most useful publication on the area. The praises of the Society's own *Mountain Flower Holidays* cannot be sung enough, for it covers selected areas where the flora is known to be interesting; and it gives references for further reading at the end of each section.

For those to whom coloured photographs are essential, there are two quite outstanding books: *Le Monde Fascinant de la Flore Alpine* by E. & O. Danesch (Didier & Richard 1981), with over 400 colour photographs, and *Fotoatlas der Alpen Blumen* by W. Lippert (Grafe und Unzer).

Travellers to the Himalayas now have Oleg Polunin's *Flowers of the Himalaya* (Oxford University Press 1984), albeit another 'heavyweight'. Formerly one had to make do with the two volumes of *Beautiful Flowers of Kashmir* by Ethelbert Blatter (Staples and Staples) and the three volumes of *Wild Flowers of Kashmir* by R. O. Coventry (Raithby Lawrence 1930).

American literature on the native flora is impossible in the kindest sense. For the traveller, most national parks have competent booklets describing some of the endemic species and these must suffice, for who can carry over 4 kilos-worth of Jepson's *Flora of California*; the 1.5 kilos of *The Flora of the Pacific Northwest* by Hitchcock and Cronquist, or the *Flora of Alaska* by Eric Hulten at 2.5 kilos!

One must stop at this point, for there are countless more titles of interest – how about the *Flora of Turkey and the East Aegean Islands* – eight volumes at £60 a piece. Not only would shelf space run out, but the finances also.

Index

Acer palmatum, 94
Aceras anthropophorum, 120
Achillea ageratifolia, 91
Aethionema 'Warley Rose',
  20
Androsace, 83
  A. alpina, 115, 117
  A. argentea, 93
  A. helvetica, 115, 116, 118
  A. imbricata, 93
  A. vandellii, 92, 115
  A. x heerii, 115
Anemone apennina, 63, 107
  A. blanda, 88, 107
  A. narcissiflora, 116
  A. nemorosa, 63, 106–7
  A. ranunculoides, 107
Antennaria dioica 'Minima', 91
Aquilegia alpina, 114, 118
Arabis ferdinandi-coburgii
  'Variegata', 20
Arcterica nana, 95
Arenaria, 83
  A. balearica, 120
Armeria, 83
  A. maritima, 78
Artemisia canescens, 91
  A. glacialis, 91
  A. pedemontana, 91
  A. schmidtiana 'Nana', 91
  A. stellerana, 91
Asyneuma pulvinaris, 84
Atragene alpina, 116, 118

Barlia robertiana, 120
Berardia subacaulis, 118
Berberis thunbergii
  'Atropurpurea Nana', 95
Bolax gummifera, 83
Botrychium lunatum, 116

Campanula allionii, 118
  C. alpestris, 69, 118
  C. carpatica, 64
  C. cenisia, 114, 115, 117
  C. cochlearifolia, 21
  C. garganica, 21
  C. 'Hallii', 21
  C. muralis, 21
  C. pusilla, 116
  C. rotundifolia, 116
  C. zoysii, 28
Ceanothus prostratus, 96
  C. pumilus, 96
  C. thyrsiflorus 'Repens', 96
Ceratostigma plumbaginoides,
  98
Chamaecyparis lawsoniana
  'Green Globe', 100
  C.l. 'Minima Aurea',
  100
  C. obtusa 'Intermedia', 100
  C.o 'Juniperoides
  Compacta', 100
  C.o 'Nana', 100
  C. pisifera 'Tsukumi', 100
  C. thyoides 'Heatherbun',
  100

Clematis marmoraria, 13
Colchicum autumnale
    'Album', 119
Colobanthus, 83
Convolvulus althaeoides, 120
    C. boissieri, 92
Corydalis, 63
Crocus banaticus, 85
    C. boryi, 85
    C. chrysanthus, 87
    C. corsicus, 88, 121
    C. flavus, 88
    C. goulimyi, 85
    C. imperati, 88
    C. korolkowii, 88
    C. kotschyanus var.
        leucopharynx, 85
    C. laevigatus, 85
    C. malyii, 87
    C. medius, 85
    C. minimus, 88
    C. nudiflorus, 64
    C. tommasinianus, 87
    C. vernus, 87
Cryptomeria japonica
    'Compressa', 100
Cyclamen cilicium, 85
    C. coum, 63, 88
    C. hederifolium, 63, 85, 88
    C. purpurascens, 116
    C. repandum, 120
        C.r. 'Album', 121
Cypripedium calceolus, 116,
    117

Dactylorhiza sambucina, 118
Daphne blagayana, 96
Dianthus, 83
    D. 'Pike's Pink', 21
    D. squarrosus, 21
Douglasia, 83
Draba, 83

Epilobium fleischeri, 115
Eranthis hyemalis, 88, 106
Erica herbacea, 95
Erinacea anthyllis, 97
Erinus alpinus, 20
Eritrichium nanum, 83
    114, 115, 116, 117, 118
Erythronium, 63, 105
Euphrasia, 113
Euryops acraeus, 90, 96

Fritillaria involucrata, 64
    F. pallidiflora, 64
    F. pyrenaica, 64

Galanthus elwesii, 86
    G. ikariae, 86
    G. nivalis 'Flavescens', 86
        G.n. ssp. *reginae-olgae*,
        86, 106
Gaultheria adenothrix, 70
    G. cuneata, 70
    G. miqueliana, 70
    G. nummularioides, 70
Gentiana asclepiadea, 108,
    116
    G. brachyphylla, 117
    G. ciliata, 116
    G. lagodechiana, 64
    G. lutea, 116
    G. punctata, 116
    G. purpurea, 110
    G. pyrenaica, 119
    G. septemfida, 21, 64, 108
    G. sino-ornata, 108
    G. verna, 116
Geum reptans, 118
Gladiolus segetum, 120
Gnaphalium sylvaticum, 113
Gypsophila aretiodes, 83

Haastia pulvinaris, 84
Haberlea, 67

H. rhodopensis, 110
Halimium ocymoides, 97
Hebe 'Carl Teschner', 95
Hectorella caespitosa, 83
Helichrysum coralloides, 96
   H. italicum, 91
   H. milfordiae, 91
   H. sibthorpii, 91
   H. splendidum, 91
Helleborus, 63
   H. corsicus, 121
   H. niger, 116
Hepatica nobilis, 107
   H. transsilvanica, 107
Hypericum olympicum, 97

Iris danfordiae, 86
   I. histrio, 86
   I. histrioides 'Major', 86
   I. 'Katherine Hodgkin', 86
   I. reticulata, 86
   I. winogradowii, 86

Jankaea heldreichii, 28, 117
Juniperus communis
   'Compressa', 100

Kelseya uniflora, 83

Lamium maculatum, 91
*Leucanthemum
   hosmariense*, 90
Leucogenes leontopodium,
   90
Leucojum aestivum, 106
   L. vernum, 88, 106
Leucothoe keiskei, 97
Lewisia, 110
Lilium croceum, 117
   L. martagon, 118
Limodorum abortivum, 120
Linaria alpina, 118
Linnaea borealis, 109

Lithodora diffusa, 97

Mimulus glutinosus, 97
Morisia monanthos, 120

Narcissus sp., 87

Ophrys fusca, 120
   O. lutea, 120
   O. sphegodes, 120
   O. tenthredinifera, 120
Origanum dictamnus, 92
Ornithogalum arabicum, 120
Oxycoccus macrocarpon
   'Hamilton', 96

Paeonia russii, 120
Pancratium illyricum, 120
Parnassia palustris, 113, 116
Petrocallis pyrenaica, 118
Petrophytum hendersonii, 98
Philesia magellanica, 97
Phlox douglasii, 20, 64
   P. subulata, 20, 64
Physoplexis comosus, 117
Picea abies 'Little Gem', 100
   P. glauca 'Alberta Globe',
   101
   P.g. 'Laurin', 101
   P.g. 'Tiny', 101
   P. leucodermis 'Schmidtii',
   101
   P. mugo 'Humpty', 101
   P.m. 'Kissen', 101
   P. sylvestris 'Frensham',
   101
   P.s. 'Gold Medal', 101
Plantago nivalis, 92
Polygala chamaebuxus, 109
Polygonum vaccinifolium, 22
Potentilla arbuscula, 97
Primula allionii, 83, 118
   P. auricula, 108

P.a. balbisii, 116
P. denticulata, 107
P. florindae, 107
P. geraniifolia, 63
P. glutinosa, 10
P. japonica, 107
P. juliae, 108
P. marginata, 67, 108, 110
P. minima, 10, 83
P. polyneura, 63
P. x *pubescens*, 67
P. rubra, 67
P. veris, 108
P. vialii, 108
P. vulgaris, 108
Prunus glandulosa
    'Albiplena', 96
P. prostrata, 96
P. tenella, 96
Ptilotrichum spinosum, 98
Pulsatilla vernalis, 115
Pygmaea pulvinaris, 83

Ramonda, 67
R. myconi, 110
R. nathaliae, 110
Ranunculus aconitifolius, 116
R. glacialis, 116
Raoulia, 84
R. australis, 91
R. hookeri, 91
R. x *logani*, 92
Rhododendron canadense, 95
R. dauricum, 96
R. moupinense, 96
R. mucronulatum, 96
R. nakaharae, 97
Rhodothamnus chamaecistus,
    117

Sagina boydii, 83
Salix arbuscula, 94
S. lanata, 90

S. x *boydii*, 94
Sanguinaria canadensis, 108
Saturea subspicata, 64
Saxifraga, 21, 83
S. biflora, 114, 118
S. florulenta, 17
S. longifolia, 119
S. oppositifolia, 114, 116,
    118
Sedum acre, 78
S. cauticola, 22
Serapias cordigera, 120
S. lingua, 120
Shortia, 109
Silene acaulis, 83
S. vulgaris ssp. *maritima*, 78
Soldanella, 109
Sorbus reducta, 98
Spiraea japonica, 98

Tanacetum densum, 90
T. herderi, 91
Thuja occidentalis
    'Caespitosa', 101
T. orientalis 'Aurea Nana',
    101
Trillium, 63
T. erectum, 105
T. grandiflorum, 104
T. luteum, 105
T. nivale, 105
T. sessile, 105
Tsuga canadensis, 101

Ulmus parviflora 'Pygmaea',
    95

Veronica bombycina, 92
Viola calcarata, 115–16
V. cazorlensis, 119

Zauschneria californica, 22
Zenobia pulverulenta, 97